THE PSYCHODRAMA

THE PSYCHODRAMA

A Play in Three Acts

David B Churchill

THE PSYCHODRAMA

© 2018 David Churchill

All rights reserved. No part of this book may be reproduced or transmitted in any form or by any means, electronic or mechanical, without written permission from the author, except for the inclusion of brief quotations in a review.

Cover art: "People's Park" by Robert Altman
Book layout by Barbara Shaw

First Edition

Published by:
Pony One Dog Press
PO Box 30552
Bethesda, Maryland 20824

*To every thing
there is a season,
and a time to every purpose,
under heaven.*

    The Byrds, "Turn, Turn, Turn" 1965

CHARACTERS

FELIX GROENEWOADE *Psychiatrist, a survivor of the concentration camps, in his late-seventies*

SARAH PANDEL *A patient, eighteen*

VIVIAN PANDEL *Her aunt, also in her seventies*

PRESTON MURPHY *A patient, late twenties and gay*

PAMELA PARKER *A patient, mid thirties*

AARON ADAMS *A former patient, in his twenties*

DIETRICH HEIDENREICH *Psychiatrist, also a former German, colleague of Dr Groenewoade's*

ROLAND LELAND *Cellist, occupies the ground-floor apartment, in his twenties*

ELEANOR GLASS *An elderly woman in the neighborhood*

KEVIN BELL *New Patient Number One, A young man in his twenties*

MAHER KESSLER *New patient Number Two, an older man, also a survivor*

Also various Workmen, Suburbanites, "Existential" People, Band Members, a Neighbor, a Nurse and a Nurse's Aide, a Priest and an Altar Boy, a Waiter, Restaurant Patrons and Office Workers. Members of the theater audience are used for the Psychodrama audience.

SYNOPSIS The past and future overlap as a psychiatrist in a down-at-the-heels neighborhood in 1960's Washington DC contemplates closing his practice, forcing his remaining patients to adjust to the end of their time together. Their struggles become acute as their lives are swept up in the changes of a new age that was dawning in America.

NOTE ON PSYCHODRAMA Psychodrama is an active and creative therapeutic approach that uses spontaneous dramatization, role playing and dramatic self-presentation to help patients gain insight and work through problems. During the Sixties, some therapists invited the public to observe psychodramatic presentations in their offices. I observed one during that time, but the one portrayed here is in no way a description of that event. In fact, I don't think there are any words that can describe the one I saw.

NOTE ON PRONOUNCIATION Throughout the play the name "Groenewoade" is pronounced many different ways. Most people pronounce it "Greenwood"; Dr Groenewoade's patients simply call him "Doctor G"; sometimes it is pronounced like German "*Grünwald*"; Dr Groenewoade himself pronounces it "*Groan-vald*."

THE PSYCHODRAMA

ACT ONE Scene One
Sidewalk outside Dr Groenewoade's house
6 a.m. mid-April, late 1960's

The sound of hammering and nails being ripped out of boards as the lights come up. An old Victorian row house appears. WORKMEN are replacing a sign in front of it.

It is early on a spring morning. A "Room for Rent" sign shows in one window nearby, another is cracked and filled with plants. As if to advertise the presence of the neighborhood's newest inhabitants, a VW parked at the curb looks as if it had been decorated by Peter Max.

The first floor windows behind the WORKMEN are uncurtained; the room within is bare save for a single chair in front of the windows. The curtains are still drawn on the floors above.

The song "Turn Turn Turn," by the Byrds mingles with car horns, birds, other sounds of a city on a Saturday morning.

From time to time throughout the scene other neighborhood figures appear, mostly old people bundled up as though it were still winter, carrying grocery bags or pulling shopping carts, evidence of the neighborhood's picturesque desuetude.

GROENEWOADE—(*emerging from the door in pajamas and bathrobe; a cat runs out at his feet and makes a dash down the steps. He speaks with an accent.*) What's going on out here! – Oh. Another sign.... (*He comes down and looks at the new* sign the WORKMEN *have propped up against the fence.* What's this one say now?

(The sign the WORKMEN *are removing is so old it's no longer legible. One end has fallen down among the weeds. They toss it unceremoniously over the fence.* DR GROENEWOADE *reads the new sign aloud:*

COMING THIS SUMMER – FROM THE LOW $200's
PHONE DU8-8893
CONDOMINIUM SALES AND INFORMATION

GROENEWOADE—So, it's true. They're going to renovate me out of my office again. *(To the* WORKMAN *who takes the sign from him)* Do you know how long that other sign's been here? Forever! That's right. Since 1950 they've been trying to run me out of here. Do you think just because you take down one sign and put up another it will happen this time? *(A young man in a tuxedo appears. He's bare-foot, carrying a cup of coffee and his shoes, a cello in a cello-case slung on his back like a guitar. He is whistling tunelessly.)* Ah, Mr Leland. Another late night? *(As the new arrival pauses.)* See what they're doing? Another sign. This time I think they mean business.

ROLAND—*(drops his shoes and cello-case and hands his cup to* DR GROENEWOADE*)* Did we get something in the mail about this? *(He goes up the steps to the mail-boxes. One hangs open, stuffed with mail. Scooping it out, he comes back down tossing bills left and right. Finding the envelope he's looking for, he tears it open and reads.)* Da da da da… "first option to purchase…" Hmm… "June 30th…" We have to be out of here by June 30th.

GROENEWOADE—Two months!

ROLAND—When was this mailed? *(Looking at the postmark.)* This was mailed two weeks ago. Why didn't you tell me?

GROENEWOADE—How am I to know you don't open your mail?

ROLAND—You can see I don't open my mail! Why would I open my mail? I don't get mail. All I get is junk.... Oh, who cares? *(He throws the letter with the others)* In two months I'll be somewhere else anyway—annoying someone *else* with my music.

GROENEWOADE—I don't complain about your music.

ROLAND—Yes you do. All the time.

GROENEWOADE—Only when I'm in session, I ask that you don't play. It's distracting, that's all. Why don't you play during the day?

ROLAND—*(Hoisting his cello and going up the steps)* I sleep during the day.

GROENEWOADE—*(Calling after him:)* I'll wager when you moved in you didn't think you'd have to move out again so soon!

(ROLAND goes in. Moments later he reappears behind the windows of the first floor. He can be seen moving about for a while, then disappears. In the meantime, an old man in a wheelchair

rolls up to join DR GROENEWOADE *on the sidewalk. He is dressed for the cold in a hat with earflaps and a long scarf.)*

NEIGHBOR—*(Swiveling about to face the audience)* Uh-oh! What's going on here? *(He's carrying a newspaper under his chin which he now takes in his hand).* I heard a racket coming from your end of the block. So it's true, they're trying to run you out again. That's what I thought. I said to myself, they're trying to run him out again!

GROENEWOADE— They're waking up the dead. No one can sleep.

NEIGHBOR—I knew they were replacing your sign. I said to myself, they're replacing that sign in front of Dr Groenewoade's house again *(he pronounces it "Greenwood").* I'll be next. They'll run us all out. Oh well, maybe it doesn't mean anything. How long was the old sign up, three years?

GROENEWOADE—Five years. Maybe ten—who counts? I've been living on borrowed time my whole life.

(One of the WORKMEN, *with the new sign on his shoulder, swings around, clipping* DR GROENEWOADE *on the back of the head.)*

GROENEWOADE—Hey you, look out with that thing! It's not enough you have to deface my house with a sign—you have to hit me with it too!

FIRST WORKMAN—Sorry, boss.

NEIGHBOR—*(Wheeling out of the way)* Well, now you have a new sign. Good for another ten years.

GROENEWOADE—And a letter, too. This time they sent a letter.

NEIGHBOR—A letter? What does it say?

GROENEWOADE—Put down a deposit—or vacate.

NEIGHBOR—That doesn't sound good.

GROENEWOADE—This time they mean business.

NEIGHBOR —Well, the neighborhood's changing. Again. It won't be the first time. *(As if to illustrate his point, a group of young people appear on the sidewalk and go silently past.)* Look at these kids. There's life in the old neighborhood yet.

GROENEWOADE—(G*etting out of their way).* Existential people! In my day we had existential people too. We called them *"Swing Jungende"*.

(The WORKMEN *too have stopped to watch the young people pass. Wolf whistles ring out.)*

FIRST WORKMAN—Hey, sweetie! Are you a girl or a boy?

SECOND WORKMAN—Hey, why don't ya get a haircut!

(The young people exit, ignoring them. One of the girls exits doing a cart-wheel.)

GROENEWOADE—*(To the* WORKMEN*)* Go back to work, you! —And make sure that sign is straight, too. Not falling down like last time. Make sure it stays up!

NEIGHBOR—What are you going to do? You rent two floors.

GROENEWOADE—Twenty years ago I needed two floors.

NEIGHBOR—Maybe you should have bought.

GROENEWOADE—Twenty years ago I wasn't going to stay.

NEIGHBOR—*(Wheeling aside for the WORKMEN again. They are finished. Gathering their tools, they depart, dragging the old sign behind them.)* I feel sorry for the others . . . For Mrs Glass, for myself . . . I'm on a pension. Thirty years in the public schools. —Where would *I* go if they decided to turn *my* building into condominiums?

GROENEWOADE—I'm in the same boat.

NEIGHBOR—But you're not retired. You still see patients.

GROENEWOADE—Only three left!

NEIGHBOR—Still, you can always move.

GROENEWOADE—With only three patients? They're poor like me! Would they drive across town?

NEIGHBOR—And the psychodrama, what will become of that?

GROENEWOADE—No more psychodrama!

NEIGHBOR—Tonight is the night, is it not?

GROENEWOADE—It is.

NEIGHBOR—You should charge admission.

GROENEWOADE—*(Scowling)* Psychodrama is not a circus.

NEIGHBOR—So many people come. So popular.

GROENEWOADE—It's therapeutic. Good for them. Good for the patients, good for the people who come.

NEIGHBOR—Like the people in the park on the weekend? So many you can hardly move. None of them live here. They come from the suburbs.

GROENEWOADE—I don't care where they come from. Too many people! *(He picks up the cat which has reappeared now that the WORKMEN are gone and turns to go in).* One of them can buy my apartment.

NEIGHBOR—It's their fault. No more room for us.

GROENEWOADE—I'm too old. Change is for the young. Custer and I will fend for ourselves. To be like the cats, that's the idea. Someone will always feed them. I'll be like an old cat too.

NEIGHBOR—*(Calling up after him as he ascends the stairs)* I almost forgot! Can you go and see Mrs Glass today? She's asking for you.

GROENEWOADE—Mrs Glass? What is it this time?

NEIGHBOR—She's having pains.

GROENEWOADE—Tell me something I don't already know.

NEIGHBOR—She's been miserable all week.

GROENEWOADE—She should go to the hospital.

NEIGHBOR—Traveling pains again. They start in the small of her back, go up under her arm…

GROENEWOADE—I'm not that kind of doctor.

NEIGHBOR—Of course she knows that. She's just lonely. She calls to me every time I go out. "When is Doctor Greenwood coming? The pains are worse. I haven't been able to eat in two days!"

GROENEWOADE—She's a foolish old woman!

NEIGHBOR—You know her cat ran away, don't you, the old tom?

GROENEWOADE—Old Jelly Bean, her favorite?

NEIGHBOR—Probably lying in an alley somewhere, paws up.

GROENEWOADE—Everybody needs a place to die.

NEIGHBOR—So can I tell her you'll come?

GROENEWOADE—I'll bring Pidark. Not Custer. Custer's not so friendly. She likes Pidark. He'll cheer her up. Tell her I'll come later.

(*The* NEIGHBOR *waves and rolls on.* DR GROENEWOADE *goes in.*)

Curtain

ACT ONE Scene Two

Dining-room in Mrs Glass's apartment.
Later. the same morning.

ELEANOR GLASS *lies on a couch that has been made up into a bed. A breakfast tray and the morning papers litter the blankets. The chairs and the dining-room table have been pushed to the side and the table is piled with groceries, plates, glasses. The rest of the furniture is old and dusty; stacks of books and newspapers make it almost impossible to get in the door. The effect is like a flea-market. Black-out curtains cover the windows; except for a little sunlight around the edges, the only illumination comes from a couple of lamps by the couch.*

(There is a knock on the door.)

GROENEWOADE—*(Outside)* Eleanor? It's me, Felix. Are you decent?

ELEANOR—*(Hastily straightening herself)* Come in!

(The door slowly opens and DR GROENEWOADE *looks in. Scott McKenzie's* If You're Going to San Francisco *can be heard behind him.* DR GROENEWOADE *struggles in, carrying a cat-carrier. With the door closed again, the music subsides.)*

GROENEWOADE—*(Pulling a chair to the side of the couch and placing the carrier on it)* Look who's here.

ELEANOR—*(Clapping her hands)* Did you bring me a visitor?

(DR GROENEWOADE clears the tray and newspapers off the couch and places the carrier on her lap.)

GROENEWOADE—*(Unlatching the door)* Hello kitty. Look where you are. Come out and be friendly. *(To ELEANOR)* I brought Pidark. He heard you needed cheering up. *(To the cat in the carrier again)* Come on kitty, you've been here before. You know Eleanor. *(A big white cat comes out and immediately runs under the couch.)* Pidark! Come back! *(He gets down and starts looking under the couch.)* Kitty kitty kitty. Not very sociable!

ELEANOR—*(Waving for him to get back up)* He'll come out. Let him be. There are treats on the table.

GROENEWOADE—*(Moving the carrier off the couch. He places a can of peas and some old newspapers he found under the couch on the table, sits down and takes her hands)* I heard Jelly-Bean's gone missing.

ELEANOR—*(Piteously, with a hand on his arm)* Have you seen him?

GROENEWOADE—*(Sadly)* No, no sign. Bob told me.

ELEANOR—That bad kitty! He never did anything you wanted him to! Just like a child! Now he's been gone for a week. Good riddance! He'll be the death of me yet.

GROENEWOADE—He'll turn up. You know how cats are. He's probably just down the block. I always told you he had more than one family.

ELEANOR—He just came in the open window, twelve years ago, made himself right at home, just as nice as you please. Chased out my other tom, Mr Whiskers, made himself right at home in his place… *(With her hand on his arm again)* You *will* let me know if you see him, won't you? Even if something's happened?

GROENEWOADE—Of course, of course. *(Patting her hand)* Bob tells me you're not feeling well?

ELEANOR—Bob? Oh, that busy-body. Whatever could he have meant by that? Of course I'm feeling fine. Never felt better in my life!

GROENEWOADE—*(Pretending to be suspicious)* How's your blood pressure?

ELEANOR—Better than yours. And I'm twenty years older. Melanie checks it twice a day.

GROENEWOADE—And your sugar?

ELEANOR—Normal, normal, normal. She checks that too. I haven't had a sweet in months. She's got me on a diet.

GROENEWOADE—Well, I'm glad to hear it. I was worried for nothing.

ELEANOR—*(Pleased with herself)* See! Fit as a fiddle. *(She takes a huge breath and goes into a coughing fit)*

GROENEWOADE—*(Making himself comfortable)* And how are things going otherwise? Is Melanie treating you any better?

ELEANOR—Oh, I wish you'd have another talk with her. I can hardly manage her anymore. You better not come near me with those needles, I keep telling her. She's a sadist! She practically admitted it. You'd better sit still, Mrs Glass, —or, I'll get you in your sleep! I'm afraid to close my eyes. —She complained so much about the closet, I had to give her the bedroom!

(There's a knock on the door. A girl in a nurses aid uniform sticks her head in.)

NURSE—I'm about ready to leave, Eleanor. Is there anything you need before I go?

ELEANOR—Come and give me a kiss, dear. *(She sits up to get a kiss on the cheek.)* I was just telling Doctor Greenwood what a terror you are with those needles of yours.

NURSE—Oh you were, were you? Well, you better watch out. *(Pinches her arm teasingly.)* I'll stick you both! Anyway, I'll be back around six, so you better be ready. —Hi Doctor. How are you this morning?

GROENEWOADE—Good morning Melanie. Off to work?

NURSE—I have a six-hour shift today, then two-hours in class. See ya later!

GROENEWOADE—*(As she exits)* This is her last year, isn't it? She should be graduating this summer?

ELEANOR—Yes, and not a moment too soon! Then the agency will have to send me someone else.

GROENEWOADE—Who was the young man who answered the door?

ELEANOR—Young man—? Oh, him. I forget his name. I call him "Boy." He's my new house boy. Just like Melanie, totally worthless!

GROENEWOADE—He seems nice enough… Only his music is a little loud.

ELEANOR—He does the cleaning and the shopping. I put him in the closet, where Melanie used to be. He makes the best scrambled eggs!

GROENEWOADE—Where does *he* go to school?

ELEANOR—I have no idea. Melanie keeps him in line. Tell you the truth, he's totally unreliable. *(Leaning forward and lowering her voice again)* I believe he's one of those, what they call "*Hippies.*" *(Sitting back again)* I don't know where they get these people. *(She winces suddenly, grabbing at her chest.)*

GROENEWOADE—Eleanor, what's wrong?

ELEANOR—*(Panting)* It's nothing. *(She picks up a magazine from the bedspread and fans herself.)* Indigestion.

GROENEWOADE—*(Standing, taking one of her hands)* Are you sure? You don't look too good. White as a ghost.

ELEANOR—I'm an old woman. My husband is dead and my children have deserted me. How good should I look?

GROENEWOADE—Your children are in Israel, silly!

ELEANOR—*(Making a face)* They want me to join them. Can you imagine? How can they expect me to go there too? I'm a sick old woman.

GROENEWOADE—I think I should call an ambulance.

ELEANOR—I'm fine, I'm fine, thank you. Ah! Heartburn—

GROENEWOADE—Well, I'll come back again tomorrow. In the meantime you better get some rest. *(He returns to the couch and picks up the cat-carrier)* I'm still not sure you look that well. *(He peers under the bed.)* Here kitty kitty kitty.

ELEANOR—Wait, don't take Kitty. Let me have him for a while.

GROENEWOADE—Are you sure? He's not being very sociable today.

ELEANOR—He'll come out when he's good and ready. Just you go on. As soon as you're gone, he'll come out and make friends. He'll keep me company till Jelly Bean comes home.

GROENEWOADE—Of course. I'll leave him here then. *(He takes her hand, which he kisses.)* I'll stop in and check on you again soon.

ELEANOR—*(Clutching his hand with both of hers)* Oh what an angel you are! What would I do without you? What a loss it would be for all of us if anything happened to you! *(She looks up at him anxiously, as though with a premonition.)*

GROENEWOADE—*(Kissing her cheek)* Calm yourself,

Eleanor. Nothing's going to happen to me. Everything's good, everything's good.

(ELEANOR *beams.* DR GROENEWOADE *opens the door, carrying the cat-carrier with him. Dylan's "Subterranean Homesick Blues" can be heard.* DR GROENEWOADE *winces.)*

GROENEWOADE—*(Above the level of the music)* Good morning, Eleanor. I'll see you again tomorrow.

ELEANOR—Good morning, Doctor.

Curtain.

ACT ONE Scene Three

Dr Groenewoade's drawing-room
Eight o'clock the same night

DR GROENEWOADE sits in the chair at his desk; his patients, PRESTON MURPHY *and* PAM PARKER *sit around a coffee table, one on a low couch, the other on the floor.* PAM *and* PRESTON *are both dressed casually,* PAM *in jeans and with a pony tail;* PRESTON *looking like a young Tab Hunter in an open collar and slacks. The couch is under the lights; the rest of the office shadowed.*

Tonight is psychodrama night. As the scene opens, spectators are arriving. They come in and spread out around the walls behind the patients, sitting along a piano bench and filling the rest of the available chairs. There's room on the couch and finally a few pick up their courage and sit cautiously beside the patients.

Finally VIVIAN PANDEL, *looking like someone out of Diaghelev's Ballets Russ, veiled and wrapped in a cape, her ghostly face rouged and made-up like an old-time actress, makes an entrance Her niece* SARAH PANDEL *with her. In contrast to* PRESTON *and* PAM, SARAH *is very stylish in a colorful pop-art dress. Together, she and* VIVIAN *make a rather theatrical pair. After leading her to the couch and depositing her in the middle with a kiss,* VIVIAN *retreats to a chair in a corner. She wields a long-stemmed cigarette-holder like a paint-brush.*

The drawing-room itself is more or less typical: bookcases, pictures on the walls, furniture of a style that was popular in the

Fifties. There is of course the usual quantity of clocks. Not so usual perhaps are the gifts donated over the years by grateful patients: mardi-gras masks, children's drawings, religious icons. They decorate the room like crutches at the grotto of Lourdes. A few actual crutches are also in evidence. One of the items is a small mirror in an ornamental frame. DR GROENEWOADE's *personal tastes include a collection of African art, also on the shelves.*

A constant noise of shuffling, coughing and whispering comes from the on-lookers. The parks, restaurants and cafes of the down-at-the-heels neighborhood have become the new "hip" destination, including DR GROENEWOADE's *drawing-room. The suburbanites have arrived for a taste of something hip.*

In the upper panes of the window the stylized fronds of the stained-glass window shine above DR GROENEWOADE's *desk, lit by the streetlight outside. The window is a casement type and its lower panes stand open.*

ON-LOOKER—(*poking his head in the door,*) Is this the psychodrama?

(*More* ON-LOOKERS *are arriving. Every time the room settles down, someone else arrives.* DR GROENEWOADE *and his therapy group wait patiently. People slip in, whisper, find places to watch from.*)

(*Someone comes in with a chair from the hallway. More shuffling, moving aside. A cat slips in and jumps on the desk;* DR GROENEWOADE *corrals him and tosses him down again.*

While they are waiting VIVIAN PANDEL *blows streams of cloudy fog thoughtfully into the room from her cigarette.)*

ON-LOOKER—(*to another* ON-LOOKER, *whispering,*) Down the hall, on the right.

(DR GROENEWOADE *clears his throat. This is the signal for something to begin. Another* ON-LOOKER *comes in.)*

GROENEWOADE—*(Ignoring the new-comer)* Sarah, would you like to begin tonight?

(SARAH *looks away and doesn't answer.)*

GROENEWOADE—Pam, you would like to begin?

PAM—As if! *(Obviously not)*

GROENEWOADE—*(As if growing impatient)* Preston, do *you* have anything to say tonight?

PRESTON—*(Shaking his head)* No—

GROENEWOADE—You've been monopolizing our sessions recently. Two sessions now, not letting anyone else talk.

(Donning a pair of sunglasses, PRESTON *does a good imitation of being an on-looker.)*

GROENEWOADE—Now is your chance. No one will interrupt.

PRESTON—*(Demurring)* It's complicated.

GROENEWOADE—Show us.

PRESTON—You wouldn't understand.

GROENEWOADE—(*Indifferently*) Okay. No matter. No one talks tonight. (*Clapping his hands*) No psychodrama tonight! Psychodrama cancelled! Everyone, home!

PRESTON—(*Jumping to his feet*) Fine! I'll show you!

(*He pulls* PAM, *who rises reluctantly, to her feet and positions her on her back in the middle of the floor. Then grabbing a bell from* DR GROENEWOADE'S *desk, he puts it in her hand and has her hold it straight up over head. Then he chases the onlookers off the piano bench and places that over her. Next he pulls* SARAH *to her feet, who also resists, and up onto the bench with him.*)

(PAM *has been ringing the bell at* SARAH *since* PRESTON *put it in her hand and now as he jumps down again to grab a carnival mask from the bookcase,* SARAH *snatches it out of her hand.*)

SARAH—You're making me crazy with that!

PRESTON—(*Trying to snatch it back*) Hey! Give her the bell!

(PAM'S *now grabbing at* SARAH'S *ankles from beneath the bench*)

PAM—(*Mockingly*) Sarie, I'm stealing your boyfriend….

PRESTON—(*Wresting the bell from* SARAH) Stop it! You're messing me up! (*Thrusting the mask into her hands*) Put this on!

SARAH—No! (*She puts it on then shoves him off the bench, almost toppling herself trying to keep* PAM'S *hands off her ankles. To* PAM) Leave me alone, slut!

PRESTON—*(After making a few more attempts to get his "characters" to do what he wants, finally has a temper tantrum)* I can't *do* this! What do you expect from me!

(SARAH *has produced a police-whistle and as* PRESTON *climbs back up on the bench, she blows it through the mask in his face. As* PAM *continues taunting her, she attempts to stomp on her hands. With the bell back in her hand, she throws it up at* SARAH.)

(*The scene devolves into a brawl.* PAM *knocks over the bench and the onlookers are sent scrambling as the scuffle escalates. The bell goes flying in one direction and the whistle in another. Cries of* YOU ALWAYS DO THIS TO ME and FINE—LETS DO *YOUR* PSYCHODRAMA *ring out. There is hair-pulling and shrieks. Through it all,* DR GROENEWOADE *sits behind his desk, impassively smoking. Finally someone makes an escape and the door slams behind them.*)

(*Silence falls over the room. For a moment no one moves.* PRESTON, PAM *and* SARAH *slowly recover themselves, try to pretend nothing has happened. Finally, extinguishing his cigarette,* DR GROENEWOADE *claps his hands decisively. He motions for everyone to leave. The psychodrama is over. No explanations are offered.*)

(*As they file out,* DR GROENEWOADE *wipes his forehead. It's hot in here. He opens the window again. People are in a hurry to leave. As the room clears, things get back to business. His patients gather, still out of breath.*)

GROENEWOADE—*(Picking up his appointment book)* Pam,

I got your message. You're cancelling your appointment next week. What day did you want to change to?

(PRESTON comes to his side also, breathing hard. They check their appointments. VIVIAN makes a motion for SARAH to wait for her outside, then remains alone as everyone leaves. The cello is audible again.)

VIVIAN—*(As the door closes behind him)* Merde! *(Her hand is shaking.)* This is a setback! *(DR GROENEWOADE sighs and lowers himself in a chair. He seems to know what is coming. VIVIAN paces.)* Why does this have to happen now? Has it finally come to this? *(She tries to light another cigarette, breaks it trying to put it in the holder and throws it down.)* After everything I've done, to die with this on my conscience?

GROENEWOADE—Vivian, you're catastrophizing. Psychodrama is supposed to be upsetting. Otherwise it's no good. We'll find out what's going on.

VIVIAN—*You* know what it is!

GROENEWOADE—*I* do? I know what it is? What is it you think *I* know?

VIVIAN—They are *all* upset. Couldn't you feel it tonight? We heard them on the sidewalk when we arrived. Where is the psychodrama? There, at the house with the sign in front. —The sign *you* allowed them to put up! *(At this DR GROENEWOADE grimaces, shaking his head "no". Behind his desk, VIVIAN pauses at the window. Cello music fills the silence. She looks down at the sidewalk)* Look at her. She's down there, waiting for me. It's spring and there's something in the air.

How much longer? Already I can feel it, pulling at her. She barely listens anymore. Everything's falling apart.

GROENEWOADE—My god Vivian, she's almost nineteen…

VIVIAN—*(Pacing again)* I, who was once an intimate of Man Ray's— I knew everyone in those days. Picasso, Cocteau, I knew them all. My writings were published in all the avant-garde presses. *(Pausing in front of the mirror on the bookcase. She adjust it the better to see herself)* Make it new, that's what they said. Make *what* new—the past, the old, the decrepit, the discarded? *(Adjusting her turban in the mirror. She is completely bald.)* We knew what that meant!

GROENEWOADE—*(Impatiently, as though the comment had been meant to marginalize him somehow)* Yes, yes, we were all young then….

VIVIAN—Make *life* new, that's what it meant! Make every day new, every moment. Make every experience new. Make *art* new! That was how we lived. And don't forget what I did for you! Look at me now, an old woman—and under a death warrant at that! How many more months are left to me? *(Turning away again)* I am a relic of myself. *(She closes her eyes and rises up, breathing deeply as if inhaling something ineffably sweet)* Ah, we were young for so long! But it is not for ever— *(She picks up a crucifix from the bookcase)* —Who gave you this? Was it that Reverend what's-his-name you were treating, the pedophile? Don't tell me you cured *him*!

GROENEWOADE—*(He takes it from her and puts it back on the bookcase).* You didn't know him. He was before you came.

VIVIAN—Don't be ridiculous. Everyone knew him. *(As he turns away, she takes it up again, paces with it clutched to her chest. Almost to herself)* We're all pedophiles and perverts…

GROENEWOADE—*(Putting his hands over his ears)* If you want to talk like this, make an appointment—

VIVIAN—You'd like to have me for a patient, wouldn't you? How would you diagnose me? Neurotic personality with inverted sexual function? *(Without waiting for an answer)* My life is over—*hers* has not yet begun. I have tasted what I wanted—*she* has tasted nothing. I, who was her guardian. To have this thrust on me.

GROENEWOADE—Why not give up these fears of yours? Let her develop normally. Let her be herself.

VIVIAN—*(Bangs the crucifix on the desk and glares at him. Then, seeing he has been silenced, continues as before, pacing again.)* My poor idiot brother. The big businessman—not a penny for his only child! A pauper. He died a pauper! And this is what I have been left with, a good death and a clean conscience snatched from me. For what? Because of a single temptation? Because for one moment I was weak? Who has not been weak? I had strength enough to save *your* life!

GOENEWOADE—*(Painfully)* You saved my life.

VIVIAN—And I would again, if the risk were a million times more. Because that's who I am. I have danced on the tightrope. Live to the fullest, the danger and the pleasure. That was my creed.

GOENEWOADE—Yes, yes…

VIVIAN—You, with your yellow star… You would have been ashes, nothing but ashes. You would have been literally less than the shadow of smoke…

GROENEWOADE—*(Resentfully; he might have survived without her help)* Some survived…

VIVIAN—So now what I did was nothing?

GROENEWOADE—Of course not. I only meant—

VIVIAN—*(Interrupting again,)* It is the sun, that star of yours, I said. Add rays around it, wear it in a sunburst. But no, you went about like a mouse, ashamed of it, humiliated. Would you be ashamed to be a star in the sky? You were terrified! That was the way you treated life… *(Quietly, at the window again.)* To have made so many errors, and not cared. But to have made *one*—and not to have been able to repair it!

GOENEWOADE—It's only a phase. Something's upset her. She's over emotional.

VIVIAN—*You* upset her—with the damned sign! *(Pressing up to him now and gazing into his eyes, the crucifix still in her hand)* The risk is too great. You understand that, don't you? Tell me, please. You understand that?

GROENEWOADE—*(With resignation)* I understand . . .

VIVIAN—I have done more to help you than you will ever know.

GROENEWOADE—*(Tiredly)* You don't need to remind me…

VIVIAN—*(Turning away again)* I feel it coming. Tests, always more tests. This time I feel it. I don't need any more results. It's a race to see which one will kill me first, the cancer or the treatment. Two devils, fighting over one carcass. It doesn't matter anymore. I've made up my mind. No more chemicals. I'm a relic of myself, a husk, a rind. Why cling to the rind when the juice is gone? I want to die as I lived. *(With a shuddering intake of breathe, listening to the music.)* Ah, listen! How that young man can play! *(In a rapture.)* A poet with strings. What *is* that music? It seems I almost know it. I have heard it all my life, only not known it! How lucky of you to have him below you! *(DR GROENEWOADE moves to close the window.)* No— Let him play. Such music of a life-time, coming from such a young man…

GOENEWOADE—It is really a nuisance—

VIVIAN—Young people—whatever one may say about them—do you think they know, in their bones somehow, all *our* sins, our evil thoughts, our ugliness's? Our stench and bad-breath? Our betrayals? Or do you think they really are like roses that grow on a dung-hill, new and fresh, perfumed with their own innocence? Sometimes in their eyes I have seen the shadows of such wisdom, not even they themselves know they have it. And if one dies, young, and has never lived—never sinned—is it all expunged then, all of it, for all of us, truly cleaned out at last…? *(DR GROENEWOADE is visibly disturbed by this. He goes back to his chair, sits and lowers his head to his hands as though he can barely hold himself up.)* And you—! *(Rounding on him now)* I know what you're thinking. Everyone knows! They see the sign at your front door and they know— *(Angrily, as DR GROENEWOADE makes a dismissive gesture)* What are you going to do? Would you take out a mortgage at your age? Do you even have any money—from these patients who don't even pay you?

GROENEWOADE—*(Faintly) You* pay me…

VIVIAN—*(Ignoring him)* Or do you plan to move, somewhere cheaper, uproot your life, move your practice?

GROENEWOADE—Naturally it would be difficult…

VIVIAN—Difficult indeed—you will leave me in the lurch. And Sarah! And the rest of the pitiful souls you've been leading to salvation all these years.

GROENEWOADE—You know me better than that…

VIVIAN—You will do what I would do in your situation. To hell with us! You've worked hard, earned a rest! Yes, you *must* retire! It is the only solution. Take what little you have squirreled away and decamp!

GROENEWOADE—Absurd— *(But with waning conviction.)*

VIVIAN—*(With a tone of bitter triumph)* You will leave and I will die and they—they will inherit! Ah, brave new world of the young! What a world we will leave them! *(At the window again, looking down.)* I must go. She'll run away if I don't keep my eye on her. Every minute is precious. Forgive me if I don't waste another one with you.

GROENEWOADE—*(Back at his desk.)* I want to see her next week. *(Checking his appointment book)* Next Tuesday, ten a.m.

VIVIAN—Impossible. I have another appointment that morning. She accompanies me on all my appointments. I am completely dependent.

GROENEWOADE—Wednesday, then…

VIVIAN—Not next week. The week after. I'm sure whatever it is, it will keep. If not, I will call. *(She pauses at the door, realizing she still has the crucifix in her hand. She looks at it a moment, then throws it back)* Here, take your testimonial! You are a good practitioner. Sarah's life will be *my* testimonial.

(VIVIAN goes out. DR GROENEWOADE remains standing by the desk, holding the crucifix. In the silence the music swells again. Finally he seems to hear it and moves to the window as if to close it, then pauses. Listening, something seems to envelop him. The music is so mournful, so sad. One of those intakes of breath seizes him, lifting him as it had VIVIAN PANDEL. DR GROENEWOADE is left alone among the upturned furniture of his office.)

Curtain

ACT ONE Scene Four

Sidewalk outside Dr Groenewoade's house.
Two a.m. the same night

The house is dark. Illumination comes from the street-light and an ornamental globe above the front door. The stained-glass panel in the window on the second floor still manages to be faintly lit from within. The VW at the curb from the first scene is gone.

(ROLAND LELAND enters carrying his cello. He is dressed as before in a tuxedo. Going up the steps, he fumbles for his keys, then pauses, frowning. Finally he looks over the balustrade into the space below, in front of the basement door.)

ROLAND—Hello? Is someone down there?

(SARAH emerges from under the stairs. She's changed her clothes and now appears wearing a mini-skirt.)

SARAH—Hello…

ROLAND—What are you doing down there?

SARAH—I wet myself.

ROLAND—You look familiar. Are you one of the…? *(He points to the apartment upstairs.)*

SARAH—*(Nodding)* I'm waiting to see Doctor G.

ROLAND—Do you have an appointment?

SARAH—I'm in crisis.

ROLAND—Oh? *(Sets down his cello.)* What's the crisis?

SARAH—Can you turn around first? Please?

ROLAND—Why?

SARAH—I need to take something off. *(He obliges and she slips out of her underpants, then hesitates. What to do with them? Finally she gives them a toss. They fall across the nearby sign and drape there. She wipes her hands on the leaves of the hedge and comes up to the foot of the steps.)* That's better.

ROLAND—Crisis solved?

SARAH—Can you let me in now?

ROLAND—No.

SARAH—Why not?

ROLAND—I don't know you.

SARAH—I'm Sarah, Sarah Pandel. What's your name?

ROLAND—Roland.

SARAH—Roland what?

ROLAND—Roland Never-Mind. *(Perching on balustrade)* Do you spend a lot of time lurking about in basement doorways?

SARAH—*(Coming part way up)* I heard your music tonight…

ROLAND—Did you?

SARAH—It's very beautiful.

ROLAND—Thank you.

SARAH—It upsets Doctor G.

ROLAND—So he's told me.

SARAH—What were you playing?

ROLAND—Something by Elgar. I don't remember.

SARAH—I've never heard of him.

ROLAND—You like classical music?

SARAH—Not really.

ROLAND—Elgar's work is usually more inspiring.

SARAH—It made me feel sad.

ROLAND—Life is sad.

SARAH—Do you play with an orchestra?

ROLAND—Sometimes. If I'm lucky.

SARAH—What do you mean?

ROLAND—I'm a floater.

SARAH—What does that mean, a floater?

ROLAND—I pick up work here and there, receptions, weddings…

SARAH—*(Interestedly)* Were you at a wedding tonight?

ROLAND—I played a bar-mitzvah.

SARAH—Where are you from?

ROLAND—Everywhere… Nowhere…

SARAH—Where do your folks live?

ROLAND—Where do the dead live?

SARAH—You're an orphan too?

ROLAND— …Mentally, yes.

SARAH—Well, I'm the real thing. I'm *physically* an orphan.

ROLAND—Is that why you have to see a shrink?

SARAH—Are you going to let me in now?

ROLAND—No.

SARAH—Why not?

ROLAND—I don't want you lurking around in the hall, outside my door.

SARAH—I won't! If he doesn't answer, I'll leave. I promise.

ROLAND—I don't trust you.

SARAH—What're you going to do when they kick *you* out?

ROLAND—Why, because of that? (*Indicating with a nod of*

the head the sign in front of the building.) I don't know… Another apartment, another city…

SARAH—Lucky you.

ROLAND—What's *your* story? —Besides being a patient of the head-shrinker upstairs.

SARAH—That's rude. He's not a head-shrinker.

ROLAND—He's not, eh?

SARAH—Did you know he was in a concentration camp?

ROLAND—I know he has a brass plaque on his door, and he's been here almost forever. And he takes in all the stray cats in the neighborhood. And sometimes I hear screaming and people throwing furniture around!

SARAH—He has a number tattooed on his wrist. *(Raises her wrist)* Right here. Number thirteen or something.

ROLAND—Is that why you go to him?

SARAH—*(Pausing)* You know, I don't think I like you, Mr. Roland Never-Mind.

ROLAND—*(Standing up)* Well, I can't stand here all night ticking you off—no matter how much fun we're having…

SARAH—Wait! Don't go yet. *(Quickly thinking of something else to keep him listening)* My parents died when I was ten. They were killed in a car accident. I don't remember much about them. Daddy was rich. His name was Chapman, Chapman Pandel. They called him Bucky. Maybe you heard of him. You would have, if you came from Virginia. He owned a lot of businesses, car dealerships, supermarkets mostly. Vivian—she's my aunt—she says he was broke when he died. She took me in. She raised me. We're too poor for me to go to college. I still live with her. Now *she's* dying...

ROLAND—What's wrong with her?

SARAH—Cancer.

ROLAND—I'm sorry—

SARAH—Can I come in *now*?

ROLAND—You're too crazy to come in!

SARAH—I had a heart-attack when I was thirteen. I died three times. Two times they brought me back. The third time they almost didn't.

ROLAND—Did you see the light?

SARAH—Everything! Looking down on yourself, the tunnel, the light. I had all that. I saw them trying to save me. Then I entered the tunnel. The light was so beautiful, so peaceful...

ROLAND—What made you come back?

SARAH—I saw Troy Donahue. He said, Sarah, I love you, but you can't die yet. Go back. So I did. They gave me a new heart. Want to see?

ROLAND—Wait. You saw Troy Donahue?

SARAH—Yep. Look at my scar…

ROLAND—I don't think he's dead yet.

SARAH—I saw him. *(As he continuous staring at her askance, she nods assertively)* Anyway, they gave me a new heart. Want to see? *(She unbuttons her blouse, showing the scar down her chest. She's not wearing a bra.)* The scar goes all the way to my navel.

ROLAND—Impressive!

SARAH—Stop looking at my breasts!

ROLAND—*(Checking himself)* Oh, yeah, that's an impressive scar, too.

SARAH—You men are all alike! *(She buttons her blouse again with an annoyed expression.)* You could be arrested for making a pass at me.

ROLAND—Really—?

SARAH—Well, maybe not literally. But if the police knew I have the heart of a little girl in me, you might. *(She experiments with her posture, trying to minimize the size of her breasts)* They gave me the heart of a little girl. Doctor G says I couldn't know that because they don't tell you whose heart you get, but I do. I asked the nurse in the recovery room what happened. She said you got a new heart. I said so I'm going to be okay? She said yes you'll be fine. I said thank God. She said yes thank God. Thank God a little girl died tonight. I said what do you mean? She said there was a car accident two blocks from here and a six-year-old girl died. They gave you her heart.

ROLAND—Well, wasn't that helpful of her!

SARAH—I used to be flat as a dance floor. (*Cupping her breasts*) Now I have breasts. Sometimes I don't know what to do with them. They grew after surgery. I thought it must have been something they did to me. (*She pauses, looking down at herself*) They told me I could never have children. It would be too much of a strain. That's when Vivian started bringing me here. She and Doctor G are old friends… Please let me in.

ROLAND—*That's* why you're seeing a shrink! Your breasts are too big!

SARAH—Isn't that enough?

ROLAND—(*Impatiently*) Go home. Come back when you get a real appointment.

SARAH—I can't… I'm afraid.

ROLAND—Afraid of what?

SARAH— …I don't know.

ROLAND—*I'd* be afraid, a defenseless girl like you, alone in the dark street. This isn't the safest neighborhood in the city.

SARAH I'm used to it, I guess. I know this street like the back of my hand. Behind you, in the doorway, I scratched my name in the stone. Many nights I come here, knock on the door, knowing it won't open, waiting anyway, sitting on the steps.... Somehow I'm not so afraid when I'm in the doorway. I think all the people on the street must know me. One of these nights he'll wake up and find me, and I'll be dead. I don't feel so alone, thinking that.

ROLAND—*(Standing again abruptly)* Well, I've enjoyed talking to you, but I have to go in. I have a busy day tomorrow looking for work.

SARAH—*(Panicky)* Wait!

ROLAND—Sorry—*(SARAH jumps up and snatches the keys from his hand. He chases her down the steps)* Hey— Come back here with those! *(He grabs her. They struggle for the keys.)*

SARAH—*(Trying to throw them)* If I can't go in then you can't either! You'll have to stay out here too!

ROLAND—*(He wrests them away As he mounts the steps again, out of breath)* There's nothing wrong with you. You're as crazy as everyone else!

SARAH—Wait a minute, wait a minute!... —I forgot your name. What's your name again?

ROLAND—That makes us even. I forgot yours too.

SARAH—You haven't told me anything about yourself!

ROLAND —I don't want to. Now go home!

SARAH—It's not fair! You know everything about me!

ROLAND—Good night. *(He wrestles his cello through the door and it closes behind him.)*

SARAH—*(Shouting at the closing door)* Play your music again! *(A moment of silence follows. He doesn't hear her. Then a click as ROLAND, on the inside, makes sure the door's locked.)* Shit…

(SARAH stares at the empty doorway. In a second the light in the front room comes on and ROLAND can be seen inside. SARAH backs away on the sidewalk to watch him, but the light goes off again. For a moment she stands alone on the sidewalk. She shivers as if cold, hugs herself. She looks up and down the street, slowly returns to the steps and resignedly climbs them. At the top she turns and sits down again, leaning against the doorway. It is too late for music. The street is silent.)

Curtain

ACT ONE Scene Five

The kitchen in Dr Groenewoade's apartment
Earlier that night, after the Psychodrama

DR GROENEWOADE is alone in his kitchen. The window on the fire-escape is open. The kitchen is full of cats. They cover the counters and the table-top, where bowls of cat food and water have been placed out. DR GROENEWOADE talks to the cats as he opens more cat-food cans and cleans the bowls and pours more milk and water. The kitchen is filled with the sound of meowing. The rumble of purring can also be heard. The light under the range hood is the sole source of illumination.

GROENEWOADE—*(To the cats as they prowl across the table, bat at each other and rub up against his legs)* Where is Jelly-Bean? Has anybody seen Jelly-Bean? Come on, kitty. Where's Jelly-Bean? –Hey you, stop that. *(Picking up a quarrelsome cat and moving it to another place on the counter)* You come over here. There's enough for all. No need to fight. You'll get yours. Come in, come in… *(As another cat appears in the window)* Have you seen Jelly-Bean tonight? Not telling eh? Is Jelly-Bean dead? His mother misses him. No one wants to talk, eh? *(He continues petting and calling the cats by name, in no particular order.)* Come here, Pepper, Shalamanezar, where's Shrike? There you are. Hello Karma and Donkor, Thom and Thomka. Come here, my kitties of the alley, Artizabal, Pixie, Underfoot, Kitty, Tibble, Blitzruff, Kit-Kat, Zebaztibal, Balthazar, Hannibal, Melchizedek…. *(Lapsing into German as the past begins coming back to him)* *Wo ist meine kleine Kätze? Wo ist mein Kätchen, mein Nikki?* *(A long sad pause follows, then)* First they took my profession.... —Passed a law, no more professions for Jews. But what of that? No more patients, no more work. But you can't take work from a doctor. They paid me whatever they could, potatoes, old shoes. a little packet of sugar—worth more than gold!... —Then they took my car. No Jews can own a car. But what of *that*? A car is only a car. I had it in for repairs more times than I drove it. Take my car, you have set me free! It was a poor car anyway.... —Then they took my house. No Jews can own houses. Take my house then, if you want it. My library, in boxes! All Jews must live together. Three rooms, then two rooms, then one room. But what of that? Every day more Jews disappeared. Soon there was room for everything again. Still they did not break our souls! *(Another long pause)* If it had just been me. No wife, no children. What could they do to *me*? Take my life?... —But then a new law. Was there no end of new laws? The devil himself was making their laws!

(He picks up a cat and buries his face in its fur.) My little Nikki, his tail in the air, like a flag. Your brother died, but I saved you. Eyes not even open yet. How I loved your carefree tail, your happy little tail in the air... Ah, Nikki, where are you...? *Wo ist mein liebes Kätchen...*

Curtain

ACT TWO Scene One

An expensive restaurant
Noon, about a week later

DR GROENEWOADE sits alone at a table for two. Behind him are potted plants and a landscape in an ornate frame on the wall. In his plain, slightly old-fashioned coat and tie he looks out of place and is obviously uncomfortable in such a fashionable setting. The sounds of a busy restaurant at lunch time do little to put him at ease. WAITERS, WAIT-STAFF *and other* PATRONS *pass as if oblivious to his presence. A single long-stemmed rose decorates the middle of the table.*

(As the seconds pass he glances at his watch. A WAITER *refills his water-glass. A* WOMAN *bumps his table, spilling his water, apologizes, goes away laughing.)*

HEIDENREICH—*(Entering in a hurry)* Felix, dear friend! Sorry to keep you waiting. Have you ordered already?

(In contrast to DR GROENEWOADE, DR HEIDENREICH *is well-dressed and at home in this environment. The younger of the two by at least a decade, he already has a pronounced tan and is rested-looking. A double-breasted suit has been tailored to accentuate his fitness. He is about a foot shorter than the older man. He too speaks with a German accent.)*

GROENEWOADE—*(Standing, bumping his water glass again)* Thanks for coming. *(They shake hands.)*

HEIDENREICH—(*Pulling out his chair and sitting down*) Sorry for the delay. Involuntary commitment. You know how those things take. The case ahead of us ran long.

(*DR HEIDENREICH spreads his napkin on his lap. DR GROENEWOADE's napkins is still on the table. A WAITER appears almost immediately. He spreads DR GROENEWOADE's napkin on his lap for him.*)

HEIDENREICH—(*To the waiter*) Glass of Perrier please, no ice. (*To DR GROENEWOADE as the waiter departs*) This is on me—no, no, I insist.

GROENEWOADE—But it was I who invited you.

HEIDENREICH—I wouldn't think of it. It's such a pleasure to see you. A celebration. My treat. It's been a while, hasn't it?

GROENEWOADE—Well, if you insist. Thank you.

HEIDENREICH—I absolutely insist. (*The waiter returns, pours more water, hands them menus. DR HEIDENREICH hands his back without looking at it.*) I'll have the endive salad with balsamic vinaigrette dressing. Bring the dressing on the side please.

GROENEWOADE —(*Also closing his menu, rushed*) I'll have the club sandwich.

WAITER—Very good.

HEIDENREICH—(*Raising his glass as the waiter departs*) Well, here's to the old country, the Fatherland. *Deutschland über alles, eh?*

GROENEWOADE—*(Tersely, nevertheless touching* DR HEIDENREICH's *glass with his own)* As long as it's not the Horst Wessel song.

HEIDENREICH—*(Laughing crudely)* Better the Internationale than that, eh? *(He pulls out a gold cigarette case, offers it to* DR GROENEWOADE *who declines, selects a cigarette himself, lights up, blowing a cloud thoughtfully across the table into* DR GROENEWOADE's *face.)* So, what is this urgent matter?

GROENEWOADE—I am in a little situation.

HEIDENREICH—Not your health again, I hope?

GROENEWOADE—No, still sound, knock on wood. *(Pulling up the table-cloth, he knocks on the table underneath.)* No, not that, but you see, I may lose my office-space.

HEIDENREICH—Really? How so?

GROENEWOADE— I ah… I received notice my building is being converted to condominiums.

HEIDENREICH—Ah…. *(Exhaling again. He continues smoking through-out and blowing the smoke across the table. It's the old psychiatric trick: don't say anything until the patient before can't stand the silence any longer.)*

(Through-out the scene other PATRONS, *passing through the restaurant, recognize* DR HEIDENREICH, *stop and greet him,*

shake hands, pat him on the back. Not everyone pauses long enough for introductions.)

HEIDENREICH—*(Sitting again after shaking hands with one of them)* Patient of mine. Typical Type A. Seven heart-attacks. He knows the next will be his last. A real challenge. You were saying?

GROENEWOADE—About my situation…

HEIDENREICH—Yes—?

GROENEWOADE—Yes, well. Naturally my first concern was for my patients.

HEIDENREICH—Yes. You have a large practice.

GROENEWOADE—Not so large… Well, tell you the truth, not many left at all. Only three still with me.

HEIDENREICH—Ah yes, I remember. I covered for you last year, when you were in hospital.

GROENEWOADE—Yes. Almost a month. Complications…

HEIDENREICH—A very attractive young woman, if I remember… (*He has a perhaps less-than ethical appreciation for attractive female patients.*) A case of post-transplant—

GROENEWOADE—*(Interrupting him, but seeming not to notice his interest)* —Yes, she is one of the three.

HEIDENREICH—Hmm. I'll have to think about it. Of course I already have a full load. I suppose I still have their addresses. The transition would be easy enough.

GROENEWOADE—If you can't take them, I'll consider another practitioner. I thought of asking you first, of course.

HEIDENREICH—Wait—only three? Last year there were four—?

GROENEWOADE—Died. One Died.

HEIDENREICH—Oh…

GROENEWOADE—A most unfortunate case. A terrible shock.

HEIDENREICH—*(Waving at his smoke and knocking ash into the ashtray next to his plate)* I'm surprised you're not used to that. People die all the time.

GROENEWOADE—*(Frowning at this, but steering the conversation back nevertheless)* I certainly don't wish anymore would die!

HEIDENREICH—Well, of course. You're not considering retiring, are you?

GROENEWOADE—That is a possibility.

HEIDENREICH—If you were planning to move, if it were only temporary…

GROENEWOADE—Not so easy, at my age. It is a difficult decision.

HEIDENREICH—*(Not holding out much hope)* I'll have to think about it…

GROENEWOADE—Oh, I forgot. Two new patients. I have two new patients. *(The WAITER reappears, removes the rose and places a basket of bread on the table. Continuing)* Five to consider now.

HEIDENREICH—Ah! *(The WAITER appears again, places their orders before them, asks if they need anything else, receives assurance that all is fine for the moment and departs. Diving into his salad)* Tell me about them, these new patients of yours.

GROENEWOADE—*(Eating more slowly)* The first is a young man. I am very puzzled by him. He spent his first appointment talking in circles.

HEIDENREICH—*(With his mouth full)* If only there were a diagnosis for that!

GROENEWOADE—Quite so. In fact I told him I didn't know what I could do to help him. He assured me I could help him very much. We shall see. I shall admit him to the group. He seemed greatly pleased at that. Perhaps the others can get something out of him.

HEIDENREICH—And the other patient?

GROENEWOADE—The other one. Yes, easier to figure out. He is an older man, a Jew. A survivor of the camps. A sort of a Nazi-hunter too, so he claims.

HEIDENREICH—*(Pausing to take a puff, skeptically.)* A Nazi-hunter? Good heavens. Are there any left? Nazis, I mean.

GROENEWOADE—I wouldn't doubt.

HEIDENREICH—*(Hastily)* Yes, yes, of course. I dare say. They couldn't have run them *all* to ground yet… Look at us. *We're* still here. *(He chuckles nervously.)* Nevertheless, I doubt *that's* why he came to you?

GROENEWOADE—I assigned a tentative diagnosis of survivor syndrome. His wife killed herself recently.

HEIDENREICH—You too are a survivor, are you not?

GROENEWOADE—Oranienburg, Nineteen Forty-Four.

HEIDENREICH—Ah, The infamous Sachsenhausen.

GROENEWOADE—Precisely.

HEIDENREICH—*(With his mouth full)* Even the practitioner too must deal with his guilt.

GROENEWOADE—Ah, yes. Guilt. The great destroyer. *(He pauses a moment, then resumes slowly, as though thoughts are still elsewhere)* Yes—. I was only there a short while, hardly long enough to experience much. Of course the so-called death march. I saw things I will never forget. To my credit I did what I could. I was not one of those who looked aside, and believe me, they were many. So at least *that* is not on my conscience.

HEIDENREICH—*(Lighting another cigarette)* No doubt there are some horrors that make the mere act of having been there to witness them a form of complicity.

GROENEWOADE—*(Quietly)* Sometimes I think merely to be alive at all is an form of complicity…

HEIDENREICH—(*Eating again.*) You were liberated by the Russians, I believe?

GROENEWOADE—The Americans. Our guards marched us out in the middle of the night. What sadists they were! You could smell the fear on them. Anyone who couldn't keep up. (*He makes a shooting gesture.*) How *I* survived I don't know. One morning we woke up. We had spent the night in a field. Everywhere, the mist, the sound of men stirring, coughing, rising from the damp ground. No food, no fires. Slowly the sun burned through the mist. It took a while to realize what had happened. We were alone.

HEIDENREICH—Incredible.

GROENEWOADE—We walked to the nearest village. All along the road, uniforms, guns, everything thrown away. The village square was full of men, everyone standing around. The same man who the night before shot a prisoner who was too weak to stand bid me *gruß Gott* as I passed him.

HEIDENREICH—(*Stubbing his cigarette out in his plate*) And you?

GROENEWOADE—I said nothing. I looked him in the eye without speaking. They feared reprisals. Not a few of the inmates themselves, too, I can tell you, the capos. Some had been worse than the guards. —Can you believe? I myself came under suspicion. I was taken for one of them.

HEIDENREICH—(*As the WAITER removes their plates*) Coffee? (DR GROENEWOADE *orders tea,* DR HEIDENREICH *coffee. The* WAITER *departs again.*) They took you for a guard?

GROENEWOADE—Not a guard, perhaps. But my condition made me suspect. I had not been in long enough to be so thin like the others. It must have appeared as though I had changed garments with an inmate. Perhaps I had been the commandant himself. The Americans put me through no small interrogation, I can tell you. I too needed a witness.

HEIDENREICH—*(As the WAITER returns with their drinks.)* You shared this with your new patient?

GROENEWOADE—Of course not. He has no reason to even know I am a Jew.

HEIDENREICH—*(Stirring his coffee.)* Nevertheless. Beware of transference.

GROENEWOADE—He will not be the first survivor I have treated.

HEIDENREICH—Well, it should make for an interesting group, whatever you decide. *(After a moment during which they have both sat silently, DR HEIDENREICH drinking his coffee, DR GROENEWOADE playing thoughtfully with his tea-bag—during which time the psychiatric "silence" seems to work in DR GROENEWOADE favor for once, DR HEIDENREICH says abruptly)* Perhaps we have all done things in the past we now wish we could change. We are old now, after all. Perhaps we were different men in the past. Take that scenario of yours, the prisoners and guards mingling in the village. Of course the SS are in fear for their lives—and not from the Americans, as you so correctly point out! Suppose then, in this scenario of yours, one of the prisoners recognizes one of his former captors. Let us even say—for the sake of argument—he was one of the more sadistic guards. He wishes him good day, hoping to pass by without being denounced. The prisoner looks in his eyes. He sees the man's fear. He sees something else, too. He sees a look that says, yes, I knocked out two of your teeth, but it could have been worse. I could have knocked out three. For the sake of that kindness, that little kindness, that tiny, microscopic, infinitesimal kindness… *(Measuring with this fingers.)* Perhaps, my friend, in that moment, both men do something they will come to regret.

GROENEWOADE—*(As if coming out of a trance)* Ach! It was nothing! *(He shakes his head, waving the idea away.)* Speculation, that is all. I don't know what occurred to me. Perhaps my new patient, the survivor….

HEIDENREICH—Stirring up old memories.

GROENEWOADE—A theoretical issue…

HEIDENREICH—Yes. Enough of the theoretical! We are men of science, after all. Let us get down to business. Of course I am ready to do anything to help, it's just that… well, as a practitioner yourself, you understand.

GROENEWOADE—Yes, well… Of course… One must keep one's practice manageable. *(He pauses.)* I suppose a trifle loan is also out of the question…?

HEIDENREICH—A loan? How much?

GROENEWOADE—*(Struggling to spit it out)* Perhaps, maybe …Not more than sixty thousand, certainly.

HEIDENREICH—*(Sitting back abruptly)* Sixty thousand!

GROENEWOADE—*(Hastily)* Out of the question! I know. Forget I mentioned it.

HEIDENREICH—Ah, I see!

GROENEWOADE—Forget it. Of course I would agree to whatever terms you demanded, but forget I mentioned it.

HEIDENREICH—But… But have you thought of a bank?

GROENEWOADE—Evidently it is not allowed to borrow money for a down payment. But don't think about it anymore.

HEIDENREICH—*(Thoughtfully)* Of course, of course… Banks have their rules. Oh dear. This *is* a problem.

GROENEWOADE— There's an end of it. I'm sorry I brought it up.

HEIDENREICH—*(He searches for an excuse)* I wish I could say this has been a better year for me. Of course I would be delighted to place a small loan with you, if it were otherwise. Problems with reimbursement. These insurance companies, always squeezing the provider… I'm sure you experience the same thing. *(He pushes his coffee away, as though to push away the request.)*

GROENEWOADE—I shouldn't have mentioned it.

HEIDENREICH—Look here. I don't care how many new patients you have acquired. Do you really want to take on a mortgage, at your age? I can understand your not wanting to retire. But think about it. You must be in your eighties by now. Is it really in your *patients'* best interests…?

GROENEWOADE—I hope everything I do is in my patients' best interests.

HEIDENREICH—Find someone else to take over your practice. True, most of your patients already know me. I already know them. I would take good care of them. Especially that young woman of yours. But so could anyone else who is competent. You think you are the only one who knows what she needs?

GROENEWOADE—Yes, some young psychiatrist just starting out, building up his practice…

HEIDENREICH—*(Signaling for the check)* Then, freedom! Do what you want. Don't get tied down at your age. That whole neighborhood of yours. Gentrifying, I believe they call it. Could you afford the taxes?

GROENEWOADE—Probably not….

HEIDENREICH—Sometimes separation can be difficult. For the therapist as well as the patient. I personally give my patients no more than five years, at most. From day one, the whole course of treatment looks to the day it ends. I tell them up front, if you are not making progress with me, you are not with the right therapist. *(He signs the bill and hands it back.)*

GROENEWOADE—Of course that's true. —Here, let me at least take care of the gratuity...

HEIDENREICH—*(Dismissing the offer)* Done!

GROENEWOADE—*(With his wallet in his hand)* Still, some of my patients are still struggling. I cannot just kick them out. It would be cruel.

HEIDENREICH—*(Smiling patronizingly)* You are a kind man.

GROENEWOADE—*(Not sure if he is being mocked or complimented)* Life is not always as clear-cut as we sometimes would like...

HEIDENREICH—Agreed. But now I must run. *(He stands up, looking at his watch)* I have a one o'clock. *(Extending his hand)* So good to see you again, Doctor. We don't meet often enough. We should get together again and go over the old days, eh? Remember, anything I can do to help. Aside from a loan, of course. And accepting your practice. Just pick up the phone. Think it over. You have earned a rest!

GROENEWOADE—*(Shifting his wallet to shake his hand)* Yes, yes. Thank you...

(DR HEIDENREICH goes out. DR GROENEWOADE absently drops his napkin back on the table, remains staring after him.)

Curtain

ACT TWO Scene Two

Private room in a hospital
The next morning

VIVIAN PANDEL is in bed, trying to light a cigarette. She is obviously drugged and sways back and forth, barely able to keep her eyes open. Over the shoulders of her hospital gown she wears a feather boa. As usual she is totally made up, heavy on the eyeshadow, but now she is totally bald. Her wig is hanging on the IV pole.

The door to the room is partially open. The overhead pager can be heard from the hall from time to time, and other sounds of a busy urban hospital.

Her niece peaks around the door, then enters.

SARAH—*(Softly)* Hi Viv. Here you are. How are you?

VIVIAN—Ah, my lover! Finally! You're a bad girl, keep me waiting so long! *(The two embrace, she comes away with smeared lipstick, resumes swaying drunkenly.)*

SARAH—*(Catching her aunt's hand that's holding the lighter)* Hey, what are you doing? What's the matter with you?

VIVIAN—*(Pulling away)* Nurse gave me something to help me sleep…

SARAH—What're you doing with the cigarette?

VIVIAN—*(Trying to light it again)* Need a smoke. Damn lighter. Worthless thing! Can't light it.

SARAH—*(Staring at her in alarm.)* I think the medicine is kicking in.

VIVIAN—Just a puff. Need a puff. Dammit! *(Cigarette is now dangling from its holder)* Where're my smokes…? *(Searching about groggily for a new cigarette.)*

(SARAH backs away, goes to the door.)

SARAH—Nurse. Nurse!

NURSE—*(Entering)* Yes?

SARAH—Did you gave my aunt something to make her sleep?

NURSE—Yes…. Is there a problem?

SARAH—She's trying to light a cigarette.

NURSE—*(Relief showing on her face)* Oh, don't worry. She'll be fine. *(Sotto voce)* I just gave her an injection of water.

SARAH—Water…?

NURSE—Yes. She doesn't have an order for anything else right now. *(Patting SARAH on the arm)* She'll be all right.

(The NURSE goes out, leaving SARAH standing there staring at her aunt in bed still drunkenly waving the lighter around, not sure what she things about the idea that as long as VIVIAN hasn't

been given a real *sleeping drug, it doesn't matter if she sets the bed on fire.)*

SARAH—*(Approaching again, more at a loss than before)* Viv…

VIVIAN—Just a puff.

SARAH—All right— Let me light it for you.

VIVIAN—No! I can do it! Goddammit!

SARAH—You're going to light the bed on fire!

VIVIAN—Need a smoke. Couldn't smoke before. That damn woman in the other bed, allergic to smoke. She's was on oxygen, for God's sake! Worried about being allergic to smoke.

SARAH—You can't smoke around oxygen anyway.

VIVIAN—That's *their* problem! I have rights too. Waited all morning to be moved! Oh, these cigarettes. Who rolled these damn things, a cross-eyed paper-hanger? How can I kill myself with these things if I can't even light one? This is torture. I can barely keep my eyes open! *(Falling back in the bed exhausted)* God, I'll be glad when it's over! How much longer must I suffer? Everything's going to pieces. I should have died years ago. Why are they doing this to an old woman who never wanted anything out of life but to be nice to people. —Nurse! Nurse! Call the nurse. How much longer can they keep me suffering like this? *(The NURSE reappears. To the NURSE)* In my purse. The envelope. Sarah, get her the envelope out of my purse.

SARAH—What is it?

VIVIAN—It's my advance…whatever. Whatever they call it. If anything happens, I am to be resuscitated! Spare no measures! Doctor G has my power of attorney.

(SARAH *gives the envelope to the nurse. The nurse looks through it.*)

VIVIAN—Stop looking at it! It's all there, all in order. Put it on my chart! (*As the nurse goes out with it*) Oh, what's taking so long with my chemo? Why haven't they come yet? I can feel those cancer cells, those perverted cells roaming through my body, eating me alive. (*Fumbling with the cigarettes again*) I can hardly breathe anymore. I'm gasping for air.

SARAH—Stop it, Viv! You're hyperventilating again.

VIVIAN—(*Ignoring her*) What did I ever do to deserve this? All I ever wanted was to be nice to people, to be a good person… (*Taking* SARAH's *hand*) Oh, Sarah, don't look at me like that. I know what you're thinking. Here I am, worrying about myself, and you're the one who's going to be left alone. My poor darling. The only ray of sunlight in my life. Look what I've done to you. (*Stroking her hair*) This is all my fault. If only my idiot brother had known how to drive! (*She turns her face to the wall*) I'm a monster. I deserve to die like this…

SARAH—(*Stoking her arm*) You're going to be fine. You're going to beat this again.

VIVIAN—(*Clapping her hand over* SARAH's *mouth*) Sssh! Don't say that. You'll jinx me. Just promise you won't let them pull the plug on me.

SARAH—Yes. Of course. But if you don't calm down, I'm going to put a bag over your head! Slow your breathing!

VIVIAN—This is the end. I feel it. The walls are closing in. I'll never leave here alive.

SARAH—*(Losing her patience. She's heard this too many times before.)* Oh please…

VIVIAN—Sarah. If anything happened to you. You're all I have left. You're so fragile. Your heart's not strong. You know that.

SARAH—Yes, I know.

VIVIAN—You have a weak heart. You have to be careful.

SARAH—I know that.

VIVIAN—Promise me you'll keep taking your medicines? Your body wants to reject your heart. Just like my body is fighting the cancer, your body is fighting your heart. One misstep and it'll kill you—

SARAH—*(Irritatedly now)* Jesus!

VIVIAN—Promise you'll keep up your appointments, not skip any appointments?

SARAH—Yes, yes. I promise.

VIVIAN—Young people think they can live forever.

SARAH—I know I won't live forever.

VIVIAN—And you'll stay with Dr G? He's a good man. He understands you. He loves you too. He loves you like the father you never had.

SARAH—I had a father.

VIVIAN—But he and I, we're your mother and father now. He knows what's best for you. Promise you'll keep your appointments with him, you won't skip any appointments?

SARAH—I promise, I promise.

VIVIAN—This whole horrible chain of events is my fault! Nurse! Nurse!

SARAH—Now what?

VIVIAN—I need the nurse. Nurse!

SARAH—I'll get her—

VIVIAN—Stay here— Don't leave me. *(Arranging SARAH's hair lovingly around her face)* Stay away from men. Men can't be trusted. They all think with their penises. A hole for their penis, that's all we are to them!

SARAH—*(A little tiredly)* I know, I know…

VIVIAN—Remember that awful boy, what was his name? That Adams fellow—

SARAH—Aaron—

VIVIAN—What he did to you! They're all like that. —Nurse!

SARAH—Poor Aaron…

VIVIAN—Don't "Poor Aaron" me! Every man you've met has let you down. That Aaron fellow was merely the worst. A real operator!

SARAH—I liked him…

VIVIAN—What a fool you are, after all! He screwed every woman in that group!

SARAH—There weren't any women in that group besides me and Pam.

VIVIAN—And you would have been next, believe me! Then off to the next group. Preying on vulnerable women!

SARAH—Well, we don't have to worry about *him* anymore—

VIVIAN—Don't use that tone, Sarah. Everything Dr G's done, he's done to protect you. And I don't care if that Aaron fellow killed himself! Just trying to get your attention. Every man you've met has let you down. Nothing but a herd of swine. Need to be run off a cliff! Thank God for Dr G! He has your best interests at heart.

SARAH—Yeah . . .

VIVIAN—But why am I lecturing you? Men don't turn your head. You're like me— We're, we're, *(searching for a term)* we're free spirits.

SARAH—*(Bluntly)* We're *lesbians*.

VIVIAN—Don't use that word! I don't like that word. That's

a vulgar word. We're, we're *Sapphics*. —Nurse! Where is that damned nurse!

SARAH—Ring the bell. Here, there's a buzzer. Push the call button.

(The NURSE reappears)

NURSE—Are you feeling better?

VIVIAN—I'm still awake. I need another shot. It wasn't strong enough. I can't fall asleep.

NURSE—I think we can arrange that. I'll be right back.

SARAH—Do you want me to leave so you can sleep?

VIVIAN—No, you stay. I don't have enough time left to spend another moment without you.

NURSE—*(Returning with another hypodermic and a piece of cotton, which she proceeds to administer after rubbing VIVIAN's arm.)* This'll do the trick. *(Wiping the injection site again)* How does that feel? I doubled the dose. You'll be unconscious in no time. *(Turning to look knowingly at SARAH)* Do you want a shot too? *(She winks and goes out.)*

VIVIAN—*(Falling back again)* Oh! Oh my God! What did that woman give me. My head's spinning!

SARAH—*(Hurriedly gathering up the cigarettes and lighter)* Close your eyes. Don't fight it…

VIVIAN—Wait! I have to pee! *(Pushing herself up again, she begins struggling drunkenly to get out of bed.)* I've got to pee! Let me go! I've got to pee!

SARAH—Jesus Christ! Viv—use the bedpan!

VIVIAN—Ugh! I threw up in it. It smells.

SARAH—*(Caught between trying to keep her aunt from falling and getting to the door to call the nurse again)* Stop— Wait! Nurse, Nurse—

VIVIAN—Where's the toilet in this room!

(The NURSE reappears in the door)

SARAH—*(To the NURSE)* Now she's trying to go to the bathroom!

NURSE—*(Halfway exasperated, halfway amused)* Don't worry. She's fine. Saline solution, remember? *(Arching an eyebrow at her)* Do I need to give *you* a shot too?

(The NURSE disappears again. In the meantime, VIVIAN has made it to the bathroom. She staggers drunkenly inside, slams the door. The toilet seat bangs. More than once. Suddenly the door explodes open again)

VIVIAN—I CAN'T PEE! *(SARAH catches her before she falls)* I can't pee! My kidneys have shut down! *(As SARAH helps her back into bed)* Oh God, my life's flashing before my eyes!

SARAH—Don't worry. I'm here. Lie down and stop fighting it…

VIVIAN—*(Groping about the bed)* Where're my cigarettes? I need a light!

SARAH—Later. Not now.

VIVIAN—*(Switching gears)* You're a good girl…

SARAH—We love each other.

VIVIAN—You take good care of me…

SARAH—We take care of each other.

VIVIAN—Don't make me worry in my grave. Take your meds. Keep your appointments. And above all—

SARAH—I know. Stay away from men.

VIVIAN—Your life depends on it. *(She tries to sing, barely gets anything out)* "First comes love, then comes marriage…"

SARAH—*(Finishing the taunt for her, but with a tired air)* "—Then comes Sarah with a baby-carriage…"

VIVIAN—*(Fading into sleep)* You'll die, Sarah. You know it… Your heart… Your heart… Your heart's not….

SARAH—Sssh. Don't worry. Go to sleep. I'll be right here…

VIVIAN—Black, everything's black….

Curtain

ACT TWO Scene Three

Dr Groenewoade's drawing room
Eight p.m. the next evening

DR GROENEWOADE sits behind his desk; PAM PARKER and PRESTON MURPHY sit around the coffee table, one on the couch, the other on the floor. PAM is dressed in long-sleeved blouse and mini-skirt, PRESTON in a tight striped sleeveless tee and bell-bottoms. Everyone is smoking. No psychodrama tonight. SARAH is not present.

There is a knock at the door, which is already ajar. PRESTON jumps up and holds it open. MAHER KESSLER, a man of DR GROENEWOADE's age, enters hesitantly. DR GROENEWOADE nods encouragingly, motions for the new patient to sit anywhere.

A clock ticks loudly. The office is full of clocks and in the silence they are a cacophony of out-of-sync ticking. The window is open and for once there is no cello playing anywhere. Only the occasional strand of music from outside and sound of traffic can be heard.

Finally the door opens again and KEVIN BELL, the second new patient, enters. He is an attractive young man with long hair, dressed in a St Pepper style drum-major's or hussar's tunic.

KEVIN—*(Looking at the space beside PAM)* Do you mind?

(PAM shrugs and looks away. As KEVIN sits, she shifts aside. She seems suddenly uncomfortable.)

(DR GROENEWOADE glances at his watch. Still no SARAH. Finally he rises and goes to a chair closer to the coffee table and joins the others.)

GROENEWOADE—Well, no Sarah. Has anyone heard from Sarah tonight? *(As the rest shake their heads)* Well, we may as well start. No doubt she will show up late. To the rest of you—and to our two new members, who haven't heard this before—this is your time and you are paying for it. If you choose not to come or must miss a session, that is your decision. But you must let me know, if you don't want to be charged. It is highly disrespectful however to waste everyone else's time by being late. *(He adds, as the others look on indifferently)* In any case I already know Vivian will not be joining us. She is in hospital again.

PRESTON—More tests?

PAM—Poor Vivian.

PRESTON—Poor Sarah. Is she with her?

PAM—I hope something hasn't happened…

GROENEWOADE—I would have heard.

PRESTON—No music, either! Where's our cello player? It's too quiet.

PAM Thank god! If I have to hear that mournful playing one more night I'll *really* go crazy!

KEVIN—*(Speaking up suddenly)* Is there psychodrama tonight?

PRESTON—No—

PAM—What do you know about our psychodrama?

KEVIN—I've been coming to them. I've been to ten.

PRESTON—I thought you looked familiar. I remember you.

GROENEWOADE—*(Remembering how difficult it had been to figure out what this young man's reason for seeking him out had been, at their initial meeting)* Very well then, Kevin. Why don't you begin by introducing yourself and tell us why you're here?

KEVIN—Well, my name's Kevin Bell—

GROENEWOADE—*(Quickly)* Please, Kevin. No last names.

KEVIN—Oh, sorry! Well, my name's Kevin. I started coming to your psychodrama last winter.

PRESTON—Why?

KEVIN—All my friends come.

PAM—So what do you think? Do we get an Oscar?

KEVIN—*(Smiling)* Yes! I want your autograph!

(PAM scowls. She stares into the corner again. After a moment she gets up suddenly, takes one of the Mardi Gras masks from the wall and returns and puts it on. She sits further away now.)

GROENEWOADE—*(Clearing his throat—as if he too finally realizes what KEVIN's motive is)* Perhaps now would be a good time to remind everyone—including our new members—about the rules. Rule number one: no fraternizing. No socializing among members. No outside friendships in group. No outside chatter. You may not speak to each other outside group. Other than in the waiting room. And you certainly may not gossip about what you hear in group. What is said in group is absolutely confidential. Anyone caught violating this will be expelled. And to your question, Kevin, as you should already know, psychodrama is only once a month.

PAM—*(Giving KEVIN a "so-there" look)* And I wouldn't do psychodrama with you anyway.

KEVIN—Why not?

PAM—I don't trust you.

KEVIN—You don't even know me.

PAM—You've been spying on us.

PRESTON—*(As if their deceased member had been caught spying on them too)* Yeah, and look what happened to Aaron…

PAM—*(Turning sharply)* Don't blame *me* for that!

GROENEWOADE—We're not blaming anyone. Aaron broke the rules. You both broke the rules. But what's done is done. *(Rebukingly, to the group)* Perhaps now we could hear from our other new member.

MAHER—*(Suddenly realizing everyone is looking at him)* Yes— *(Clearing his throat)* I am called Maher. I was a doctor before I retired. My wife died. *(He speaks with an accent.)*

GROENEWOADE—Can you tell us how she died?

MAHER—*(Slowly at first)* Well. For a long time she couldn't sleep. She had some sleeping pills. She was taking them to sleep. Then, one night I dreamt I was freezing. All night. I kept dreaming of snow, of ice… So cold. Soon I saw why. In the morning I awoke to find her beside me, standing on her head in the pillow.

GROENEWOADE—Rigor mortis?

MAHER—Just so! Of course, I didn't know what had happened. She was like a horse, so healthy. *(Thumping his chest)* More than me!

GROENEWOADE—*(Prompting. Of course he has heard this before)* What did the autopsy show?

MAHER—Pills. She had all of them in her stomach. So many! I didn't know! *(He looks down, as if overcome for a moment.)* She was planning all along. I never knew.

PAM—*(To herself)* Jesus, another suicide! *(She is still smoking, inhaling and blowing smoke through the mask.)*

MAHER—I am still seeing her in bed beside me, standing on her head. *(He presses his fists into his eyes, then shakes his head vigorously.)* Am I too so depressed, that being sad all the time seemed normal?

(At that moment a door slams downstairs, sending a gust through the room.)

PRESTON—*(Looking at the door)* Ah-ha. Late as usual!

PAM—*(Disgustedly)* Here she comes.

(But there are no sounds of footsteps on the stairs and in fact SARAH PANDEL does not appear.)

GROENEWOADE—*(Resuming)* Maher, no doubt you and your wife were both depressed, given your experiences. That would be natural. But you cannot hold yourself to blame for her death. If she had reached out to you, you would have responded, you would have stopped her, but it is clear that she had every intention of succeeding.

MAHER—But in bed, beside me! Why did she do it like that? Did she not know what I would find when I awoke? How could she have done that, if not to punish me?

PAM—Maybe she thought you would just think she had died in her sleep.

PRESTON—Think how she must have felt, to be driven to that. She might have wanted the comfort of dying beside you.

(A sudden burst of female laughter comes from below.)

PRESTON—*(Breaking the silence) That* sounded like Sarah…

PAM—Playing hooky….

(While they are speaking DR GROENEWOADE gets up and closes the door.)

PRESTON—Well, at least somebody's ready to leave the group!

PAM—*(To DR GROENEWOADE, alarmed.)* Are you retiring?

PRESTON—*I* could leave the group. I'm cured.

PAM—*(Mockingly)* You! Cured!

GROENEWOADE—Good for you, Preston. Are you ready to graduate?

PRESTON—I could be in a relationship with a woman...

PAM—*(To DR GROENEWOADE again, lifting the mask)* Did you decide something you didn't tell me?

GROENEWOADE—Nothing has been decided. I merely remark that Preston has made good progress.

PRESTON—I might still *act* like a queer, but I only do that because I choose to.

PAM—Give me a break! You've been "cured" from swinging the wrong way by swinging both ways? Anybody can do that!

GROENEWOADE—And what about you, Pam? How long has it been now?

PAM—What is this? Everybody has to be ready to leave now?

PRESTON—*(Answering for her)* Fifteen years. More than fifteen. I've been here twelve. You were already one of the old timers.

PAM—I could leave too if I wanted. I'm cured.

GROENEWOADE—You've made good progress too.

PRESTON—We're a family, growing and changing together.

PAM—Except we can't talk to each other. —Only when we're here!

PRESTON—Why should we? We already know everything about each other.

PAM—For your information I've only been here fourteen years.

KEVIN—*(To PAM) You're* not gay, are you?

(PAM doesn't answer. She pulls the mask over her face again.)

PRESTON—*(As if answering for her)* I can't have relationships with women and she can't have relationships with men.

PAM—*(To PRESTON)* Shut up!

KEVIN—*(Nodding. He has his answer.)* I didn't think so.

PAM—*You* should know. You're been spying on us.

GROENEWOADE—Only the very wealthy can afford to make therapy a life-time hobby.

PAM—Define "cured" for me. Are you cured when you don't care anymore? In that case, I'm definitely cured!

GROENEWOADE—What were the goals you set for yourself? What did you hope to accomplish?

PAM—*(Deigning to answer, after an annoyed pause)* I wanted to be in a relationship.

GROENEWOADE—Would you care to elaborate for the group?

PAM—Everyone already knows. —Let *him* tell us! *(Jerking her head toward KEVIN.)*

KEVIN—I don't remember . . .

GROENEWOADE—*(To PAM)* Humor us.

PAM—*(Drawing a frustrated breath)* Jesus—

GROENEWOADE—Take the mask off.

PAM—Christ. *(Stubbing her cigarette out)* Now you're *really* picking on me!

GROENEWOADE—Show us your pretty face.

PAM—*(Heaves another over-loud sigh, removes the mask, draws another breath again. Pauses again.)* I wanted a relationship that lasts longer than, than... than a popsicle in hell. *(The mask has loosened her hair and she shakes it out angrily out of her face. As seems suddenly apparent, she really is an attractive woman. There is an air of vulnerability about her now. She goes on in the present-tense.)* I want to stop jumping into bed with every man in a bar who smiles at me—and never calls again. I want a man to like me for who I am. —Not for what I put out....

KEVIN—*(Quietly)* There are probably a lot of men who like you and would want to be with you. *(KEVIN has either been in a few groups himself or taken especially good notes at the psychodramas he's observed.)*

GROENEWOADE—Is that true, Pam? Is what Kevin says true?

PAM—*(Looking into her lap)* Nobody who isn't a total jerk would want to be with me. If he wasn't, he'd be with someone else.

(In the silence that follows, the opening cello strains of the concerto by Elgar slowly swell into the room—breaking one spell—and casting another. DR GROENEWOADE *stirs himself, looks at the clock on his desk.)*

GROENEWOADE—Well, shall we break here? This is as good a moment as any. We can take this up next time. Next week perhaps Pam will share more with us concerning the progress she is making toward achieving her goals.

(The others stir, put out their cigarettes, rise, stretch, begin filing out. PAM *places the mask she is carrying back on the wall.)*

GROENEWOADE—*(To* PAM, *as she passes again to go out, in a voice meant only for her)* Well done tonight, Pam. *I* know you have made progress. I am proud of your openness.

(She nods—almost imperceptibly. At the door, KEVIN *seems to be waiting for her. She tosses her head as she passes.* KEVIN *follows her out.)*

*(*DR GROENEWOADE *remains standing alone, watching them. Finally he too puts out his cigarette. The cello rises as the stage darkens.)*

Curtain

ACT TWO Scene Four

Front-Room, Roland Leland's Apartment
Eight p.m. the same evening

This is the room that corresponds to Doctor Groenewoade's drawing-room on the floor above. The windows are closed. The same music and traffic sounds that could be heard upstairs are heard mutedly again. What follows is what was happening below while the prior scene was transpiring above.

The room is dark, lit only by the streetlight falling in through the windows in front, but in the light it will be revealed to be a typical crash-pad: no furniture except for a chair in front of the windows, mattress on the floor, blankets, clothes and books scattered about. A few dead plants of different sizes stand about in tin cans, dry leaves and twigs litter the floor. A garden hose hangs over the door to the back of the apartment. The walls are almost totally papered up to arm's-reach with music scores.

Outside in the hall, DR GROENEWOADE's *patients are arriving. The sound of the front door opening and closing and their footsteps going upstairs outside the apartment continues until the last patient has arrived and gone up.*

Finally the apartment door opens. ROLAND LELAND *enters struggling with his cello and snaps on the light, revealing a single bulb in the overhead chandelier. He is in his tuxedo with the tie untied.* SARAH PANDEL *follows in wide-legged pants and a bold print shirt. Both are trying to be quiet.*

ROLAND *crosses to the oppose side where, trying to put the cello down quietly, it slips from his grasp and thuds to the floor.*

SARA—*(Forgetting to close the door)* Shhh! I don't want anyone to know we're here!

(ROLAND makes a face. Then, tip-toeing, he goes to the nearest window and pushes it open. As he does so, a breeze enters into the room, stirring the leaves on the floor—and slamming the door behind them.)

SARAH—*(Jumping)* JESUS!

ROLAND—*(Making another face)* Well, I guess they know we're here now.

(They stand listening—as if they could hear anything from upstairs—then ROLAND *shrugs and opens the other windows. Behind him* SARAH *moves forward, looking around interestedly.)*

ROLAND—*(Turning to watch her)* Like my plants?

SARAH—Mmmm. I see Ali left some of his goods behind…

ROLAND—Who?

SARAH—Ali. From Tunisia. He was a street vendor. He sold plants over on Connecticut Avenue. Stored his inventory here. Used to see him sometimes loading up his van.

ROLAND—I guess that would explain the hose… *(nodding toward the hose hanging over the door behind them)*

SARAH—*(Kicking at the leaves)* What you need is a rake.

ROLAND—Where would I get a rake?

SARAH—*(Looking at him with sudden suspicion)* You're just squatting here, aren't you?

ROLAND—What do you mean?

SARAH—You're not paying rent.

ROLAND—Would you pay rent for a place like this?

SARAH—Where'd you get the key?

ROLAND—Maybe that Ali of yours—whose real name by the way is Mojtaba—is selling plants on Fifth Avenue now, up in New York. *(She reacts to this revelation silently as he pulls the chair over and straddles it, then gestures at the mattress for SARAH.)* Have a seat.

SARAH—*(Instead of sitting, she continues inspecting the room. Looking now at the sheet-music papering the walls)* What's all this?

ROLAND—My music.

SARAH—Why is it all over the walls?

ROLAND—Don't have a music stand.

SARAH—You could buy one.

ROLAND—I told you, I'm a floater. Floaters travel light.

(He takes out a pack of cigarettes, shakes one out, offers her one, then lights both. SARAH finally clears a path for herself to the

mattress and lowers herself. ROLAND *pulls one of the dead plants over to use its can as an ash tray and flicks his cigarette ash into it.*)

ROLAND—*(Exhaling again)* How's your aunt today?

SARAH—*(Also flicking ash)* Not good. *(She tilts her head sadly.)* I don't know. She's been sick a long time. But this time. I don't know…

ROLAND—Chemo not working anymore?

SARAH—*(Shaking her head)* They moved her into Intensive Care this afternoon.

ROLAND—I'm sorry.

SARAH—Every time they say the cancer is gone, it comes back. Sometimes she's in remission for a year, once for two years. She's had radiation, chemo, peach-pits….

ROLAND—Peach-pits?

SARAH—Yeah, down in Mexico. Some experimental treatment. All it did was make her break out in hives. *(Exhaling a moment)* She's had cancer almost the whole time I've been with her.

ROLAND—And no family…?

SARAH—My parents died when I was ten. I told you. Viv took me in. *(Then, with a sudden note of self-disgust)* A year later I seduced her…

ROLAND—You *what*—?

SARAH—Don't judge me.

ROLAND—*(Skeptically)* When did that happen?

SARAH—When I was eleven.

ROLAND—That's pretty young to be seducing people—especially an adult.

SARAH—Viv said that's how it happened. She said I was precocious. She said it's natural for children to have sexual feelings. Doctor G said so too. It's not like I'm a *pervert* or anything—

ROLAND—How does a child go about seducing an adult?

SARAH—We were in the same bed.

ROLAND—You got into her bed, or she got into yours?

SARAH—Well… We slept in the same bed. My parents had just died when she took me in. She let me sleep with her.

ROLAND—*(Shaking his head)* Still. Not sure that's the way most people would see it.

SARAH—I don't care what most people would see.

ROLAND—I can't believe your shrink goes along with that.

SARAH—Vivian would never molest me, if *that's* what you're thinking!

ROLAND—*(Unconvinced)* Hm!

SARAH—Then pretty much right away I started having heart

trouble. It was like a punishment from God. Then, after the transplant—you know, I started growing. *(Lighting another cigarette)* Then Viv found out she had cancer… —Don't you have anything to drink around here?

ROLAND—*(Ignoring the question)* I suppose the cancer's a punishment from God too.

SARAH—He's taking away the only person who ever loved me.

ROLAND—*(Stubbing his cigarette out)* One disaster after another.

SARAH—This time… I just have a feeling.

ROLAND—What are you going to do? If she does—you know—if she dies…?

SARAH—I don't know… I don't have a job. Vivian didn't like me working.

ROLAND—Didn't you tell me your folks were rich?

SARAH—They died broke.

ROLAND—No insurance? What about your aunt?

SARAH—Nothing.

ROLAND—That sucks!

SARAH—Poor Viv. She looked so small this morning, so old …All those tubes coming out of her. She squeezed my hand. It was all she could do. *(After smoking silently again)* I did her make-up. A little eye-shadow, re-drew her eyebrows. She doesn't even have eyebrows anymore… *(Putting her cigarette out half-smoked and reaching for another)* But enough about me. I still don't know anything about you.

ROLAND—*(Lighting her cigarette and another for himself)* Well, my parents are still living. Dad's a doctor, mom's a social worker. We're a high-achieving family. —Except me.

SARAH—You don't want to be like them?

ROLAND—I couldn't stand to be like them—but I realize that probably doesn't sound like much to someone in your position.

SARAH—You don't know Vivian and me. Viv lived in Paris and all over Europe. She believed children should be allowed to do whatever they want.

ROLAND—Another Gertrude Stein.

SARAH—Another who?

ROLAND—*(Ignoring this too)* Sounds like I could have been happy with your aunt.

SARAH—You talk as if your folks disowned you or something…

ROLAND—I disowned myself. *(Opening his cello case and returning with the cello and bow. He turns the chair around.)* A highway ran past the high-school where I grew up. On spring days I used to sit in class and look out the windows, watch the cars passing. I loved the idea of being in a car and being on that road, just driving, heading out west. Left right after my last class, a friend and I. Didn't even bother sticking around to get my diploma.

SARAH You didn't graduate?

ROLAND—I graduated. I think. But probably just barely. I just wanted to get out of there. So we took off, this girl and me. Hitch-hiked to California—by way of the rest of the country. *(He tunes the cello while speaking, cigarette between his lips.)* In San Francisco we met another couple who'd just gotten back from a year in Mexico, hitch-hiking around. So we decided to do it too. Got as far as Ensenada.

SARAH—What happened?

ROLAND—Maybe if one of us had spoken more than a couple words of Spanish it might have worked. We ended up spending a few nights freezing in the desert. Spent our last night together in a wrecked car in a junk-yard. The next morning I took everything I had and bought Natalie—that was her name—bought her a bus ticket back to San Fran. The bus passed me on the side of the road while I was still waiting for a ride. I caught a glimpse of her face looking out the window as it blew past. I think she was waving. That was the last I saw of her.

SARAH—Why…? You didn't follow her?

ROLAND—I did. Took me about a week. We were supposed to meet up again at our friends' place. But they'd already moved. When I got there some other people were living there. All I found was one word in Natalie's handwriting scrawled on the sidewalk in front.

SARAH—What did it say?

ROLAND—"Braz."

SARAH—What does *that* mean?

ROLAND—It's the name of a place in Oklahoma, a coffeehouse. Brazen Articles. We met some people there but she couldn't remember their names. She wanted me to know I could find her with them. But I had to work a while to get up more money, then a few more days to get there. Too long to expect anyone like her to wait around. She was gone again. That was two years ago.

SARAH—And since then?

ROLAND—Oh, I've seen her. In a store window, passing in a crowd, in the window of a passing bus. She got my cello out of hock at one point and left it for me with some friends. See? *(He turns it around and shows her a place on the back.)* "You owe me." Scratched it in the wood with her fingernail. *(He says this almost proudly.)* I've gotten a few letters from her, messages left on coffee-house message-boards, news from mutual friends… Whenever I heard of her in some place, I wrote. I gave messages to friends….

SARAH—You miss her very much.

ROLAND—*(Adopting supercilious tone)* Love is the greatest prison of all.

SARAH—Don't say that—

ROLAND—Have you ever met someone you felt you've known all your life? Like maybe even from another life?

SARAH—No—

ROLAND—*(Teasingly)* Like voyagers on a cosmic ocean, travelling through creation from life to life, searching for each other, every life a new chance to meet…

SARAH—I don't believe that. *(After a moment, as if falling under the spell)* Do you think we'll ever find our soul-mates?

ROLAND—*(Serious again)* I don't know. Our soul-mates are probably right beside us, and we're too blind to see. But when I find mine again, I'm not sure she'll even be the same person…. But I keep looking.

SARAH—Do you think you could ever see your soul-mate in me…?

ROLAND—(*Mockingly*) No—

SARAH—Not a chance?

ROLAND—Less chance than a Chihuahua in China.

(A peal of laughter is torn from her and just as abruptly stifled. She looks back up at him again, deadpan.)

SARAH—That wasn't funny.

ROLAND—Not meant to be—

SARAH—*(Looking grimly across the room)* I guess I don't have a soul then.

(In the silence that follows ROLAND *concentrates on the pitch of the strings he is tuning. Finally* SARAH *looks back up at him, as though she is still waiting for an answer.)*

ROLAND—*(Deigning to answer as he takes up the bow)* I guess that depends on whose heart you have inside you.

*(*SARAH's *look changes to one of coldness but she remains silent.* ROLAND *closes his eyes and soon the notes of the cello concerto begin filling the room.* SARAH *puts her cigarette out again and sits on the mattress, staring into space. She is not listening.)*

Curtain

ACT TWO Scene Five

The Pandel family plot at the cemetery
Morning, a few days later

In the background, a large head-stone with the name "PANDEL" on it, and beneath that the names "Chapman" and "Lola." In front of that stand a Catholic PRIEST *and an* ALTAR BOY, *the* PRIEST *wearing an alb and chasuble, the* ALTAR BOY *in surplice and cassock;* SARAH *stands beside them in a short black raincoat and short boots. In front of them are flowers and an open grave. There is no casket. It is raining and* SARAH *is holding an umbrella and a bouquet of roses. The* ALTAR BOY *holds an umbrella over the* PRIEST.

As the scene opens, SARAH *is staring at the ground, the* PRIEST *is smoking a cigarette.*

GROENEWOADE—*(Entering from the side, also carrying an umbrella)* Ah, here you are!

(Everyone moves over as he joins them. He looks around. They are still waiting. Finally he notices there is no casket.)

GROENEWOADE—*(In a low voice, after frowning at the open grave for a moment)* Where is the casket?

SARAH—It's a long story.

GROENEWOADE—Undertaker is lost?

SARAH—I wish.

GROENEWOADE—A mix-up with the bill?

SARAH—*(After a pause)* A mix-up at the hospital.

GROENEWOADE—What happened?

SARAH—*(Not sure if she's annoyed or just sad at the whole thing)* It's a long story. A mix-up with the death certificate.

GROENEWOADE—How so?

SARAH—Viv ended up in the Emergency Room. The Medical Examiner took her.

GROENEWOADE—*(Quietly aghast)* My god…

SARAH—*(Still keeping her voice down)* Her doctor was going out of town, so he signed the death certificate before he left. She wasn't expected to survive the weekend, and that's what they do there. But somebody new was in the admitting office, where they handle these things. Where he worked before they didn't sign anything till afterward. So when he saw that, he called the funeral home. Naturally the funeral home brought her back when they realized she wasn't dead yet. The hospital was really busy that night, beds were tight—or so they say. Anyway, the floor wouldn't take her back, so they had to put her in the ER. Next morning they found her in a back cubicle. She was dead. Didn't even know who she was.

GROENEWOADE—Where is her body now?

SARAH—*(Shrugging, suddenly indifferent)* Who knows? Cremated! Thrown in a dumpster!

GROENEWOADE—Oh my God. Poor Vivian. *(They stand in silence again,* DR GROENEWOADE *repeating "Oh my God poor Vivian" over and over. Finally)* The hospital will pay for that!

SARAH—No— They were very contrite.

GROENEWOADE—What do you mean, no? —I should say they were contrite. It's an outrage! Well they should be!

SARAH—I told them, mistakes will happen. It didn't affect Viv's well-being.

GROENEWOADE—But the indignity—!

SARAH—She would have been the first to appreciate the irony.

GROENEWOADE—Still. They should pay.

SARAH—*(Waving the idea away)* I just don't care anymore. She's been sick so long. It's time to move on. It can't *always* be about Vivian. Besides, I don't want their money. Not like this, anyway. What does it matter, in the end? It wouldn't bring her back. (DR GROENEWOADE *is clearly unsatisfied by this, but says nothing. Finally, taking a last look around,* SARAH *motions to the* PRIEST.) We may as well start. Doesn't look like anyone else is coming.

GROENEWOADE—*(Just realizing a* PRIEST *is there)* A priest—? Why is there a priest? A priest and no body.

SARAH—Don't worry. It's paid for. She wanted a funeral and she's going to get one.

PRIEST—*(Tossing his cigarette and opening his book)* If you O Lord mark iniquities, O Lord, who can stand? The Lord be with you.

SARAH—*(Dully, in response)* And with your spirit

PRIEST—Let us pray. O Lord, we commend to you the soul of your servant—

SARAH—*(To the PRIEST)* Excuse me? Can you do this in Latin? Viv loved the Latin mass.

PRIEST—Sorry. Don't know Latin.

SARAH—*(To herself)* Shit. Damn Vatican Two.

PRIEST—*(Resuming)* Let us pray. O Lord, we commend to you the soul of your servant— *(Reading from a paper pulled from under his robes)* Vivian Pandel, that, having departed from this world, she may live with you. And by the grace of your merciful love, wash away the sins that in human frailty she has committed in the conduct of her life. Through Christ our Lord.

SARAH—Amen.

PRIEST—O God, you alone are ever merciful and sparing of punishment. Humbly we pray you in behalf of the soul of your servant— *(Pulling the paper out again)* Vivian Pandel, whom you have commanded to go forth today from this world. Do not hand her over to the power of the enemy— *(A wind comes up, blowing their umbrellas.)* And do not forget her forever; but command that this soul be taken up by the holy angels and brought home to paradise, so that, since she hoped and believed in you, she may not undergo the punishments of hell— *(A crash of thunder sounds. Ducking his head)* But rather possess everlasting joy. Through Jesus Christ.

SARAH—Amen.

(A sudden downpour of rain hits.)

PRIEST—*(Struggling to stay under the umbrella)* May the Lord be with you.

SARAH—And with your spirit.

PRIEST—*(Turning to another page as the rain continues heavily)* And as we read in John, Chapter Eleven Verse 21, At that time Martha said to Jesus, "Lord, if you had been here, my brother would never have died . . . . "

SARAH—*(To the PRIEST)* Excuse me. That's enough. Thank you. I think Vivian gets the point. Thank you.

(The PRIEST shrugs, then makes the sign of the cross, stows his book and takes the umbrella from the ALTAR BOY. They leave, huddled together against the rain. SARAH and DR GROENEWOADE remain standing alone, staring into the grave. A few seconds pass in silence. The rain tapers again, continuing off and on.)

SARAH—*(Finally)* Poor Vivian. What a mess.

GROENEWOADE—She was a beautiful person.

SARAH—She deserved better.

GROENEWOADE—She was a good friend.

SARAH—She did her best.

GROENEWOADE—When she was born, she wasn't expected to live. She was premature. Her mother didn't want her. Her father said she'd never be right, if she did live.

SARAH—She didn't want to die. Don't let me die. Those were her last words.

GROENEWOADE—We all have to die.

SARAH—Poor Vivian.

GROENEWOADE—One of her aunts took her. She fed her with an eye dropper. It was a miracle she lived. *(They continue staring at the open grave in silence a moment, then DR GROENEWOADE continues.)* She had a free life.

SARAH—*(After a moment)* What do you mean?

GROENEWOADE—It's like when you have appointments on your schedule all day every day for a month. Then you wake up one day and you realize you made a mistake in your calendar. You have no appointments that day. The day is free. You can do whatever you like with it. That's the way it was for her. She wasn't expected to live, but she did. It was a life she could do anything with. Nothing she had to accomplish, no problems to solve, no challenges to face.

SARAH—*(Remembering something VIVIAN didn't have)* She

wanted a cigarette. I could have given her a cigarette. If only I'd known. It would have been the last cigarette she ever smoked, a last pleasure.

GROENEWOADE—She risked her life to save mine. She didn't have to, but she did. She was a good friend.

SARAH—Risked her life?

GROENEWOADE—This was in Germany. Many of my patients were in the arts, theater people, the like. That's how we met. She had a Swiss passport. If it was a fake or not, I don't know. She spoke three or four languages. She could easily pass as Swiss.

SARAH—She missed not traveling. We couldn't afford it.

GROENEWOADE—When I had the chance to leave, I stayed. I stayed for my patients. Then it was too late to leave. This was in thirty-nine. I was in danger of being put on a transport. Vivian had Swiss diplomatic papers. Somehow she got a marriage certificate that said we were married. She moved in with me. After that, the Nazis left me alone. For a while…

SARAH—You never told us that.

GROENEWOADE—A lot I never told you. Of course, if they had found out our documents were forged, both of us would have been shot. We lived in constant fear. Every knock on the door could have been the end. Even ordinary Germans suffered. Everything was rationed Only she got the coupons. Only she could buy food. No coupons for Jews. I lived on potatoes for a year. If only that had been all! As the husband of an Aryan my life was spared, but we were subjected to so many restrictions. Always forced to move, smaller and smaller quarters. Constantly harassing us, coming in the middle of the night, searching our apartment, our rooms. Turning our belongings upside down, breaking things, scattering everything, confiscating things they claimed were verboten for Jews. *(He stares at the open grave a moment in silence.)* Always a new indignity. *(They both stare at the grave, then DR GROENEWOADE continues.)* Finally they forced her to leave. They made up some pretext to send her back to Switzerland. That was in Forty-Four, the end of Forty-Four. I was ordered to report for transport the next day. Barely six months in a camp. Even then your aunt didn't give me up for dead. After the war she looked for me. I was in a camp for displaced persons. She brought me to this country.

SARAH—She was a good person.

GROENEWOADE—*(Looking around as if waking up, a little embarrassed to find himself having gone on so long.)* It was a bad time. People's true natures appeared. Even those who were capable of selflessness, of good, of risking their lives for others, even they harbored their own evil. People were breaking free, it was the spirit of the times, but they didn't understand. Many died, some lived—but no one was spared. *(Doctor Groenewoade turns to face SARAH. He doesn't want to just turn and walk away, but he's not sure what to do. Finally he seizes her hand and squeezes it.)* For all I may have done to you—I'm sorry! *(SARAH stares at him, surprised. Embarrassed, he corrects himself.)* What I mean is—I'll see you next week. Goodbye. Don't catch cold.

(SARAH watches him leave, then turns to face the grave again. A long moment passes. A sudden gust of rain wakes her up. With an abrupt gesture she flings the roses into the grave. It is not a gentle gesture.)

SARAH—*Auf weiderzehen,* Vivian. Thank you for everything.

Curtain

ACT TWO Scene Six

Preston Murphy's room, above M Street in Georgetown. Saturday night, the next weekend

There's no dialogue, per se, in this scene—unless you call the interplay of Velvet Underground's "Walk on the Wild Side" with the sounds of an arguing couple and a crying baby—interspersed with sounds of a woman being physically abused—coming through the wall from the next room a dialogue.

PRESTON is dressing to go out. He sits at a dressing-table brushing out a wig. "Walk on the Wild Side" is playing on a boom-box. The scene opens with the boom-box turned up and someone pounding on the wall from next door. TURN THAT GODDAM SHIT DOWN.

The windows in the back look out over the street, the sounds of the busy night-life and the traffic filtering up into his room. Across the street, neon signs for the Crazy Horse and the Cellar Door (although these venues actually didn't have neon signs) blink on and off. The other furniture includes a double bed, unmade, racks and piles of women's clothes, and a lamp with a red shirt over its shade. Theater posters of Nureyev, Margot Fonteyn and other ballet stars adorn the walls. PRESTON keeps a cigarette going in the ashtray beside him.

We watch him apply make-up, gaff himself, try on a few wigs, select one of the more outrageous pageant wigs and a party dress to go with it and finally, throwing a kiss to himself in the mirror on the dressing-table, turn the lamp off and leave.

The action consists entirely in PRESTON*'s transformation—buffeted by intermittent sounds of physical and verbal abuse coming from next door. Voices shout, doors slam, glasses break, loud crashes knock posters off the walls, a woman screams, a baby wails. The volume on the boom-box starts off at a respectable level, but as the noise from next door begins to overpower it,* PRESTON, *who mocks the violence by pretending* he's *the one being choked and knocked around, turns it up, again and again with every increase in noise, until a furious pounding awakens again shaking the wall and a man's voice bellows* TURN THAT SHIT DOWN YOU GODDAM COCK SUCKING FAGGOT BEFORE I COME OVER THERE AND SHOVE MY FOOT UP YOUR ASS, *at which point* PRESTON *turns it down and the process repeats itself.*

The implication—though PRESTON *doesn't appear to appreciate it—is clear: in transforming himself into a woman, he is entering dangerous territory.*

Curtain

ACT THREE Scene One

Pam Parker's office at the law firm of Casper Casperson
About noon, a week later.

A typical office in a law firm: law books line the shelves that cover most of the walls, a Currier & Ives print on one bare wall above a small conference table on one side; on the other PAM's desk sits in front of a window. A door stands open on a hallway where the ringing of phones, the greetings of receptionists' and other busy office sounds can be heard. A huge vase containing a dozen flowers, one of every kind, stands on PAM's desk.

As the scene opens, PAM is at her desk, speaking on the phone. She is wearing a pants suit and glasses. Her hair is up again.

SECRETARY—*(Appearing in the door.)* Excuse me, Pam. Someone's here to see you.

KEVIN—*(Pushing in from behind her. He's wearing a Greek fisherman's cap and carrying a paper bag.)* Hey Pam! Ready for lunch?

PAM—*(Covering the receiver)* Kevin? What're you doing here?

KEVIN—*(As the SECRETARY disappears again)* I'm taking you to lunch, remember?

PAM—*(Into the phone)* I'll have to call you back. *(To KEVIN, hanging up)* What lunch? You're not taking me to lunch. *(She stands, removes her glasses and comes out from behind her desk.)*

How did you get in here?

KEVIN—It wasn't easy!

PAM—So what do you want?

KEVIN—I wanted TO make sure you got the flowers.

PAM—Oh, those are from *you*? *(Reading from the card)* From your "secret admirer"…? How sweet! Have you lost your mind?

KEVIN—I didn't know what your favorite flowers are so I ordered one of each.

PAM—There's a lot you don't know about me, Kevin. They must have been very expensive. I'm just a little confused though. How'd you find out where I work?

KEVIN—I have my ways.

PAM—I'm not sure if I should feel flattered—or threatened.

KEVIN—Oh, come on. Look, it's lunch time. Let's get a bite to eat and sit in the park. On me.

PAM—I can't. —Look, I'd love to, but we're in a bit of a crunch. I can't get away.

KEVIN—Okay. Let's eat here. As it happens, I brought some lunch with me.

(PAM stares at him a moment, frustrated. Finally she seems to realize it's pointless to resist.)

PAM—Fine. A quick lunch. *(Leading him to the little conference table)* Over here.

KEVIN—*(Unloading the paper bag)* Peanut-butter and jelly… Peanut-butter and mayonnaise…? *(She reaches gingerly for the peanut-butter and jelly. Neither seems to appeal to her very much.)* Coke… Or Pepsi?

PAM—*(Resignedly)* Do you have anything diet?

KEVIN—*(Rummaging in the bag)* Iced tea.

(They unwrap their sandwiches and begin eating. Neither says anything for a moment. People hurry back and forth outside in the hall.)

PAM—*(Finally)* So. How was group?

KEVIN—Missed you.

PAM—Too busy. Big case coming up.

KEVIN—Sarah wasn't there either.

PAM—Who was there?

KEVIN—Just me and Maher.

PAM—Preston wasn't there?

KEVIN—He came and then left. Wasn't feeling well.

PAM—What was wrong with him?

KEVIN—I don't know. Looked like he'd lost weight.

PAM—Hope it's not serious. *(She eats in silence a moment)* Did Doctor G figure out what he's going to do yet?

KEVIN—About moving? No. The sign's still there.

PAM—There's always been a sign there.

KEVIN—I guess he'll figure something out…

(The SECRETARY comes in again, carrying a stack of folders.)

SECRETARY—Pam, Bill asked if you could look these over when you get a chance. They have to go out today.

PAM—Just put them on my desk. Thanks.

(The SECRETARY goes out again, pausing to get a whiff of the roses on the desk. She catches PAM's eye on the way out and raises her eyebrows.)

PAM—*(To KEVIN as the secretary goes out, annoyed)* So, Mister "I've-Got-My-Ways". Aren't you afraid *you're* going to be kicked out of group when Doctor G finds out you came over here?

KEVIN—Is that the worst that could happen?

PAM—The last person who broke that rule died.

KEVIN—Whoa! Who was that?

PAM—Aaron—.

KEVIN—Aaron! Everybody talks about Aaron. Aaron this and Aaron that! What happened?

PAM—Long story. Don't have time to tell it.

KEVIN—All right.

PAM—You know Sarah's story, right?

KEVIN—So are we going to gossip about everybody now? I thought that was forbidden too.

PAM—Might as well. Can't throw us out twice!

KEVIN—So what about Sarah—other than she's a dyke?

PAM—If she's a dyke I'm the Pope's shaved-ape love-child.

KEVIN—That older woman, who always comes with her…?

PAM—Her aunt.

KEVIN—What's *her* story?

PAM—I don't know. She's not really supposed to be there. She's not in group.

KEVIN—Why does Doctor allow it—aunt or no aunt?

PAM—*(Signaling her ignorance with a shake of the head)* Does that seem right?

KEVIN—*(After a moment)* If he's going to break the rules for one person, what's the big deal if the rest of us break a few too, now and then?

PAM—Good point.

KEVIN—Why do keep going to him?

PAM—Why do we *all* keep going to him? *(She eats silently a moment, then as if drawing out a reluctant confession.)* We feel safe with him.

KEVIN—I don't think you should feel *that* safe. It's therapy after all, isn't it? Getting better isn't always comfortable.

PAM—*(Reflectively)* Sometimes a safe place is what you need…

(A male COLLEAGUE *appears in the doorway, notices* PAM's *busy, makes a "call me" sign and goes out.)*

PAM—*(Nods to her* COLLEAGUE, *then continuing to* KEVIN*)* Anyway, I think Aaron got caught up in that craziness. *(Looking at* KEVIN's *paper bag)* What else do you have in there?

KEVIN—*(Rummaging around again)* Crackers…? *(As she takes the crackers and begins opening them)* So what happened?

PAM—Sarah is guy-crazy. I think that's the real reason she's in group, why her aunt is always with her, won't let her out of her sight. Won't let her cross the street by herself. *(KEVIN produces a packet of Ding-Dongs and unwraps it, offering one to* PAM, *who takes it)* Doctor G put down every guy—who wasn't gay, of course—who joined the group. You think it's tough talking about your feelings in group, then having everyone beat up on you? He went out of his way to make every guy who so much as put his face in the door look like a dick—but in a professional way, you know— Like he was trying to be helpful.

KEVIN—*(Pulling an orange out of the paper bag)* Dessert? *(He peels it and they share it.)*

PAM—*(Continuing)* In Dr G's defense, you probably wouldn't want any of your female patients getting involved with any guy in that group. These guys have problems or they wouldn't be there. But I think he went too far.

KEVIN—About turning Sarah off to guys?

PAM—Like she might fall in love and get pregnant and die because her heart isn't strong enough or something. Excuse me—hasn't anybody heard of birth-control? *(She takes a piece of orange and stares at it a moment.)* Anyway, his usual tricks didn't work with Aaron.

KEVIN—No?

PAM—For one thing, Aaron was a nice guy. A genuinely nice guy. Hard to find bad things to say about him. Secondly, they really liked each other. He and Sarah.

KEVIN—So what happened?

PAM—I'm a slut, Kevin. I've fucked every good-looking guy that ever joined that group—and some not so good-looking guys, too. Doctor G knew that. *(Accepting another piece of orange.)* One day after a private session, Doctor G asked me to drop off a prescription for Aaron. Valium or something. Said he'd forgotten to give it to him and Aaron really needed it. He even gave me Aaron's address!

KEVIN—Oooh… Set him up.

PAM—Yep. Me too. He knew what was going to happen.

KEVIN—Nobody can resist you, huh?

PAM—*(Smiling wryly at the backhanded compliment. Then, knitting her brows)* Funny thing, I don't really remember very much about that afternoon. I remember driving there. I remember having some drinks…. At least one drink…

KEVIN—Maybe he was the one who came on to you?

PAM—I don't think so. I know myself too well. Besides, in the end, does it matter who came on to whom?

KEVIN—You blocked it out.

PAM—*(Thinking about it)* Well, that's what Doctor G said. Guilt and all that. But I don't know… All I remember is waking up the next morning, looking for my clothes, and leaving. *(She shrugs)* I guess I must have.

KEVIN—But killing himself? Come on.

PAM—We broke the rules. One of us had to leave. Should have been both. Doctor G gave us a break. He said one of us could stay, but we had to decide.

KEVIN—*You* could have left.

PAM—I was going to! Aaron wouldn't let me. He said he would take the blame.

KEVIN—Sure. He could have found another group.

PAM—I saw him outside on the sidewalk the next week waiting for Sarah to come out. He wanted to talk to her. She wouldn't have anything to do with him.

KEVIN—How'd you find out he killed himself?

PAM—Find out—? He did it in front of us!

KEVIN—Jesus!

PAM—Never noticed that big stain on the carpet?

KEVIN—How—shot himself?

PAM—He showed up a week later, weeping, pleading to be given another chance, pulled out a gun, started waving it around, put it up to his head— BOOM! Blood all over the room.

KEVIN—*(After a moment)* Wow! *That* would have made a great psychodrama!

PAM—That would have been the end of psychodrama.

KEVIN—Was he depressed?

PAM—Not that anyone knew. That's what made it such a shock.

KEVIN—Guilt is a destroyer. *(After a moment)* But it wasn't you, it was Dr G. He set the whole thing up. Sounds like he knew what would happen. *(Then after a moment)* —Not the suicide part, maybe, but everything else.

PAM—Still. I feel responsible…

KEVIN—*(After a moment)* Enough about him! Let's talk about us.

PAM—*(Starting to gather up the wrappers in front of her)* No, let's not talk about us. There is no "us."

KEVIN—*(Ignoring this, he looks around the office)* So you're a lawyer, huh?

PAM—Last time I checked.

KEVIN—What kind of law do you practice?

PAM—Business. Mergers and acquisitions…

KEVIN—I'm on unemployment.

PAM—You don't have a job?

KEVIN—I'm in a band.

PAM—Really? What's it called?

KEVIN—The Blues Poodles.

PAM—Where do you play?

KEVIN—In a basement.

PAM—*(Grinning)* I'll bet you don't have a record contract either…

KEVIN—Not yet.

PAM—*(Glancing at her watch)* This has been nice, Kevin, I mean that—but I *really* have to get back to work now.

(The phone rings. She gets up and answers, exchanges a few words with the caller, then hangs up again.)

KEVIN—*(Sweeping the remains of their lunch into the paper bag)* How about dinner tonight?

PAM—No—.

KEVIN—Tomorrow night?

PAM—Kevin, I gotta hand it to you. You really are a sweet guy, and I love the roses, and that you tracked me down, and brought me lunch… But I'm not going out with you.

KEVIN —Why not? Afraid you'll get in trouble with Dr G?

PAM—Kevin, how old do you think I am, anyway?

KEVIN—I don't know. Twenty-five?

PAM—Try thirty-five

KEVIN—So…?

PAM—Never trust anyone over thirty, remember?

KEVIN—I like older women.

PAM—I'm not dating you.

KEVIN —Why—because I might like you?

PAM—Yes, because you might like me—no, *not* because you might like me—I mean, yes, yes—because you might like me. I don't *want* you to like me.

KEVIN—So, I guess dinner's out?

PAM—You're not even working, Kevin. How can you take me out to dinner?

KEVIN—I make a little money now and then…

PAM—How, playing on street corners?

KEVIN—It's still money— Are you busy tomorrow night?

PAM—*(Firmly, pushing him toward the door)* Kevin, if you joined Dr G's group because you thought you could get in my pants, I'm afraid you're going to be disappointed.

KEVIN—*(With mock disappointment)* But you said you're a slut!

PAM—*(Closing the door on him)* I'm a selective slut.

KEVIN—Wait!

PAM—Goodbye, Kevin.

KEVIN—I have an idea.

PAM—*(Impatiently)* What?

KEVIN—Why don't you come over and listen to us play?

PAM—*(Letting up on the door for a moment)* You're a nice guy, Kevin, you really are. That's why I can't date you. And you *certainly* don't belong in Dr G's group. Take my advice, get out of that group. We're a bunch of sickos. Don't get mixed up with us.

KEVIN—*You're* not sick!

PAM—You haven't been listening to me, have you? *(Finally pushes the door closed)* And no more flowers, okay? I mean it! Leave us to our misery—!

(Almost immediately the door begins opening again. PAM *shoves back hard, only to be met now by the surprised face of her* ASSISTANT. *Handing her a telephone message, the woman disappears again, leaving* PAM *leaning against the closed door in exhaustion.)*

(Finally, on her way back to her desk, she sees a leftover Ding-Dong wrapper on the conference table. Scooping it up, she carries it back to her desk, where she sits staring at it, slowly smoothing it out. Then suddenly she crumples it and tosses it away.)

Curtain

ACT THREE Scene Two

Flashback. Aaron Adams' apartment
Afternoon, several years earlier

A home-movie screen lights up on stage and a projector begins whirring. A count-down sequence appears as a sixteen-millimeter film starts running. This is a flashback scene. Floyd Kramer's "Last Date" piano composition, popular in the late 50's, establishes the year. The image is flickery, the film stock old and the film poorly-edited; instead of a sound-track, the actors, out of sight, read their lines, voice-over style. They are not always in perfect synch.

The film begins with PAM *getting out of her car on the street, going into an apartment building and down a long hall. She knocks on a door. Once* PAM's *inside, the apartment is revealed to be similar to what one would find in a motel: shag carpet of the era, low beige couch, matching coffee-table, end tables with nondescript porcelain lamps with over-large lamp-shades, a low upholstered chair, also beige; across from the couch is a bar sans bar-stools with a refrigeration and kitchen range behind it. It's obvious the apartment came furnished. There's a revolver on the coffee-table.*

AARON ADAMS, *when he appears, is an attractive young man with an effeminate, almost child-like demeanor, like a young Sal Mineo. His most outrageous expressions are delivered with a teasing slyness, like a little boy who knows he's too cute for anyone to stay mad at for long. He dresses prep-school style.*

After knocking at the door and when no one answers at first, PAM *bends down to slip the prescription* DR GROENEWOADE *had given her under the door. The carpet on the other side is too thick and the prescription won't slip, forcing her to her hands and knees. Suddenly the door opens.*

AARON—Finally! *(As Pam stares up at him in surprise)* Hi!

PAM—*(Standing finally and taking stock)* What do you mean "finally"? Were you waiting for me?

AARON—*(Throwing the door wider to let her in)* Yes! You're late!

PAM—How did you know I was coming?

AARON—*(Pleased with his own cleverness)* I looked in Doctor G's appointment book, so I knew when your next appointment was. Then I called him just before you got there, so I knew when you'd be leaving to come over here.

PAM—*(Not sure how to take this information)* Well.... I had to drive around the block a few times before I felt safe enough to park. *(Hands him the prescription.)* Take this and let me get out of here.

AARON—*(Throwing it over his shoulder)* Don't need it—

PAM—Wait! I rushed all the way over here to bring you something you don't need?

AARON—Oh, I need what you brought—but *that's* not it!

PAM—What're you talking about?

AARON *(Coyly)* What if I just wanted Doctor G to give you my address and a reason to come over? Would you be angry? *(PAM stares at him with a mixture of emotions on her face. She's starting to get the picture and it's a nice one.)* I can get him to do anything. He likes me. *(As PAM continues looking at him askance, he puts an arm around her shoulders, drawing her further into his living-room.)* Thought it would make it easier for us to get more acquainted.

PAM—*(Throwing his arm off)* We're acquainted enough—

AARON—*(As if offended)* Come on. What are you afraid of? Didn't Doctor G tell you to come here?

PAM—I'm not thinking about him.

AARON—Who then?

PAM—Your girlfriend, for one!

AARON— Sarah? I'll get to her. *(He tries to steer her toward the couch, arm on her shoulders again.)* First things first.

PAM—*(Throwing his arm off again)* I've seen the way you too have been looking at each other.

AARON—We've got a thing going, sure. So what? I like you too.

PAM—*(Backing toward the door again)* Well, count me out. I'm nobody's appetizer. —And I wouldn't do that to Sarah anyway.

AARON—Oh really? Aren't you the one who fucks all her boyfriends?

PAM—Sarah doesn't have any boyfriends. You should know that. You haven't even gotten to first base yet, and you never will. I'm just someone who feels sorry for guys.

AARON—Well, feel sorry for *me* then!

PAM—*(Laughs humorlessly, yanking the door open)* Ha! What a come on!

AARON—All right, all right! Hold up— Let me at least offer you something to drink. You came all the way over here, it's the least I can do. *(As she hesitates, he draws her by the hand toward the couch again.)* Come on, come on. Don't make me feel bad. Sit down and let me get you a drink.

PAM—All right…. Just a quick one. *(She reluctantly sits.)* What're you going to do when I tell Doctor G you tricked him?

AARON—*(From behind the bar)* Don't' worry. I'll get the prescription filled. I really have been having trouble sleeping lately.

PAM—*(Noticing the revolver on the coffee-table for the first time)* Whoa— You must *really* live in a bad neighborhood! *(She picks it up gingerly by the trigger-guard.)*

AARON—*(Laughing)* No, no. That's not what it's for. It's a toy.

PAM—This is no toy. Even I can tell this is real.

AARON—It's still a toy.

PAM—What kind of person uses a gun as a toy?

AARON—*(Handing her a drink)* You know, target practice, Russian roulette…. That sort of thing.

(Before she can react, he puts the gun to his temple and pulls the trigger. Nothing happens.)

PAM—*(Jumping as though he had aimed at her)* Shit! Don't do that!

AARON—*(Laughing)* It's unloaded. See. *(He dry fires the gun few more times.)* See, no bullets.

PAM—*(As he points the gun at her)* Holy shit! Get that away from me!

AARON—*(Still laughing, he picks up a box of bullets from the bar)* Look, the bullets are over here.

PAM—An unloaded gun is the most dangerous gun there is!

AARON—*(Putting gun and bullets back on the bar and sitting in a chair opposite her)* Ah— Seriously?

PAM—Seriously! People are always getting shot by guns they think are unloaded.

AARON—People who aren't careful…

PAM—You are so seriously going to shoot yourself. Or someone else. And don't ever point a gun at me again.

AARON—*(Pouting)* Fine, fine. I was just kidding with you.

(PAM *calms down as they stare at each other. Finally he takes a sip and she slowly follows.*)

PAM—Ptoo! What *is* this! *(She stares at the contents of her glass as though it were turpentine.)*

AARON—Rum and Coke…

PAM—If this is rum and Coke, I'm a turnip!

AARON—Actually, I'm out of Coke…

PAM—What did you use then—dish-soap?

AARON—Tab…. I was going to use Doctor Pepper but I thought you might be watching your calories.

(PAM *makes a face, closes her eyes and downs the rest.*)

PAM—*(Slamming the glass on the coffee-table with another expression of disgust)* Ugh!… Okay. Thanks. Gotta go.

(*Instead of moving, she continues to sit there, blinking, hand on her stomach. She belches.*)

PAM—Pardon me. Ugh.

AARON—Want another?

PAM—No. I gotta go.

(*Another moment passes, during which she begins having trouble keeping her eyes open.*)

PAM—What did you put in that?

AARON—Too much rum?

PAM—*(Beginning to speak with a slur)* Shit. I can drink you under the table anytime.

AARON—*(Feigning concern)* Maybe you better not leave yet.

PAM—I don't feel too good....

(PAM makes a few ineffectual attempts to stand, finally falls back, struggles to stay awake, then slowly keels over sideways.)

(AARON remains seated, sipping his own drink, staring at her. A long moment passes in silence.)

AARON—*(Finally, feigning a sigh)* Pam, Pam, Pam. What are we going to do with you? *(Swirling his drink)* Sisters before misters, huh? Such a good friend! *(Downing his drink)* I do wish we could've gotten to know each other better. I think you really would have opened up to me. So much hurt, so much pain. All that frustrated longing to connect. *(Shaking his head as he gets up)* I think you would have liked me if you'd have given me a chance. Now we have to do something, don't we? Can't leave you lying there. But what're we going to do? Decisions, decision, decisions. Should we get undressed out here—or get undressed in the bedroom? *(Pulling her to her feet)* What would *you* normally do, jumping in bed with all those lonely men of yours? Pull your blouse off in the living-room . . . ? *(Trying to keep her from falling back on the couch)* Come on, stand up. Don't make me do all the work. (*He unbuttons her blouse and drops it on the couch, then steers her toward the door to the bedroom.)* Then what happens? Leave your shoes in the hall…? *(He slips off her shoes and tosses them in the hall)* Can't wait to feel his hands in your pants…? Is that how it happens? And you know we *will* tell Doctor G all about it, won't we… *(Struggling to support her and disrobe her at the same time, he guides her to the bedroom.)* Come on now. You're not helping…

(Film-strip flares out and the screen does dark.)

Curtain

ACT THREE Scene Three

Dining-room in Mrs Glass's apartment
About ten a.m. the morning after Kevin and Pam's lunch

(NOTE: *These last three scenes blend into one another via the use of a <u>revolving stage</u>, as one scene segues into another. Also in the last two scenes the stage continues to revolve, more or less, throughout as the actors walk on it.*)

ELEANOR GLASS lies on the couch that has been made up into a bed. As before, breakfast tray and the morning papers litter the blankets. The room is the same as in Act One, dining-room table piled with groceries, plates, cups and glasses, stacks of books and newspapers piled up everywhere else. The only difference is that the black-out curtains have been pulled aside and sunlight floods the room.

The fat white cat is lying contentedly on ELEANOR's lap as she strokes and baby-talks to him. Every now and then, afflicted by tics, she shivers, raises an arm as if to call out to her aide, thinks better of it, heaves a sigh, reaches out in another direction as if for something, forgets what she wanted, twitches again, then goes back to petting the cat.

(There is a knock on the door.)

GROENEWOADE—*(Outside)* Eleanor? It's me, Felix. Are you decent?

ELEANOR—*(In a high voice, hastily straightening herself)* Come in! Come in!

(*The door opens and* DR GROENEWOADE *looks in. This time Friends and Lovers "Reach out of the Darkness" can be heard behind him.* DR GROENEWOADE *struggles in, carrying the cat-carrier again.*)

GROENEWOADE—(*Pulling a chair to the side of the couch and placing the carrier on it*) Look who I found!

(*As soon as the cat carrier is placed on the couch, the white cat stands and spits, fur rising on its tail. As* DR GROENEWOADE *unlatches the door, the cat jumps down and goes under the couch.*)

ELEANOR—(*With an expression of joyful surprise at the new arrival*) Did you find him?

GROENEWOADE—(*Pulling him out*) I found him!

(*A large tri-color tom emerges reluctantly from the carrier*)

ELEANOR—(*Grabbing him up*) My Jelly-Bean! You came home to me!

(*Jelly-Bean escapes and also jumps down. He disappears under the couch too, followed by a commotion.* DR GROENEWOADE, *on his hands and knees, drags the white cat out and places him in the carrier, then stands again with Jelly Bean and hands him back to* ELEANOR. *As she takes him, he closes the door to the room so he can't run out.*)

ELEANOR—(*To the cat*) You bad boy! You made mummy so upset. I'm going to spank you if you run away again! (*Pretend spanking, evolving into a cheek rub*) Oh, I was so worried. (*She puts a hand on her heart as though re-enacting the painful experience*) Where were you hiding, you bad boy!

GROENEWOADE—*(Petting Jelly Bean with her)* He came to my window.

ELEANOR—*(With a sigh of relief)* What would I do without you!

GROENEWOADE—I told you he'd come back when he got hungry.

ELEANOR—He went to you. He knew you would bring him home.

GROENEWOADE—*(Pulling something out of his pocket)* That's not all. Look what he was wearing! *(He hands her a rhinestone collar with a name-tag dangling from it.)*

ELEANOR—*(Taking it gingerly)* What is it?

GROENEWOADE—It's a collar. Someone else took him in. He was wearing it when he came to me.

ELEANOR—*(As though the collar would bite her)* Oh, my goodness!

GROENEWOADE—I knew you didn't put it on him. It has a name-tag on it.

ELEANOR—Oh, what does it say? *(Reading it upside down)* Elkraps— Elkraps…? *(As DR GROENEWOADE turns it around)* Sparkle… Sparkle! What kind of name is that!

GROENEWOADE—He's someone else's "Sparkle."

ELEANOR—*(Letting go of the cat on her lap as though he were suddenly radioactive)* He's not my Jelly-Bean?

GROENEWOADE—He *is* your Jelly-Bean. But he's someone else's Sparkle, too. He has another family.

ELEANOR—*(As if gasping for air)* Oh! Oh!

GROENEWOADE—He's a good cat. He's sharing himself.

ELEANOR—*(Still afraid to touch the cat)* Oh, my! He has another family! And they don't even know his name! Sparkle. What kind of name is that? He doesn't sparkle at all!

GROENEWOADE—Perhaps some young people took him in… Everything sparkles to them….

ELEANOR—He's not a cat for young people! He's an old cat. He's a cat for old people.

GROENEWOADE—Young people like old things too.

ELEANOR—*(With a snort)* They don't like old things. All they like is their music and going around in strange clothes scaring the daylights out of old people like me!

GROENEWOADE—You'll have to keep him in if you don't want him running back to them again.

ELEANOR—Oh, my! He's a devil at getting out!

GROENEWOADE—*(Stroking the cat)* At least he came home. Another family may think he belongs to them, but *he* knows where belongs.

ELEANOR—*(Gingerly touching Jelly Bean again, following* DR GROENEWOADE'*s lead, with the collar in her other hand)* To think, all those times he disappeared… Another family!

GROENEWOADE—*(Taking the collar from her and pocketing it again)* You should put your own collar on him, with his real name.

ELEANOR—*(To Jelly Bean)* What a bad boy you are! Making me think you were lost. All this time, somebody else's house!

GROENEWOADE—Alley cats always have more than one home. *(He bends down to pick up the carrier with the other cat in it.)* We're both alley cats, aren't we, Eleanor? Two old alley cats.

ELEANOR—*(Grasping his hand and looking up at him coquettishly)* Oh, you know me so well!

GROENEWOADE—*(Warmly, after gazing at each other silently a moment)* I have a new friend who'll look in on you, if anything happens to me.

ELEANOR—*(Suddenly stricken, clasping his hand tightly)* Oh, what do you mean, Felix? What do you mean, if anything happens to you?

GROENEWOADE—Now don't worry about that. In case I have to move or something. But I have a friend who'll look in on you. I've told him all about you.

ELEANOR—*(Worriedly)* Is he a nice man? I'm afraid.

GROENEWOADE—He's a very nice man, a widower. His name's Maher. He's from the old country, like us.

ELEANOR—And you, Felix? What will happen to you?

GROENEWOADE—*(Hoisting the cat carrier up)* Don't worry about me. We old cats always land on our feet. *(Kissing her hand)* I'll bring Maher to meet you next time.

ELEANOR—So is it certain?

GROENEWOADE—Nothing is ever certain. *(Pidark, in the carrier, loudly expresses his feelings about being scooped up.)*

ELEANOR—Oh, there's something you're not telling me!

GROENEWOADE—Don't fret, Eleanor. Change is good for us. *(She is fanning her chest now)* Calm yourself, or you'll move *your*self right out of here—into a hospital bed.

ELEANOR—It just seems so unfair.

GROENEWOADE—Whoever said life was fair?

ELEANOR—So unjust!

GROENEWOADE—It is we who are unjust, if we don't get out of the way. Things are just what they are. *(Kissing her hand again, he finally turns away)* Let me go now. I'll stop in again. Now I must take this big boy home before my arm breaks. *(Friends and Lovers "Reach out of the Darkness" is heard again as he opens the door.)* I must say, that young man's music is loud. *(As ELEANOR throws her arms about in a gesture of exasperation at the younger generation, DR GROENEWOADE pauses a last time, shouting to make himself heard)* Don't forget to keep our wanderer in. A few days should teach him a lesson about straying.

ELEANOR—*(Raising one of Jelly Bean's paws puppet-like to*

wave goodbye as the door closes) Say goodbye, Jelly Bean. Say come back again. I'll never run away again. That's a good boy.

Curtain

ACT THREE Scene Four

Sidewalk outside Mrs Glass's apartment
The same morning

As DR GROENEWOADE goes out the dining room door, the stage revolves to reveal him coming out of the house at the front door. A flight of steps leads down to the sidewalk. The music stops as he closes the door behind him.

As he comes down to the sidewalk, ROLAND LELAND appears, carrying his cello case.

ROLAND—*(Approaching)* Doctor Greenwood, I found you!

GROENEWOADE —Ah, the young man with a cello!

ROLAND—*(Setting the cello case down)* They told me I might find you here.

GROENEWOADE—Who's keeping track of me now?

ROLAND—Your neighbor, the one in the wheelchair.

GROENEWOADE—That one! He's such a busybody.

ROLAND—I didn't want to leave without saying goodbye.

GROENEWOADE—Leaving? Who's leaving now?

ROLAND—I am. I'm leaving. No more practicing my music to drive you crazy. I'm going.

GROENEWOADE—Going? Going where?

ROLAND—I don't know. Just going. Time to travel on.

GROENEWOADE—Before the workmen return, eh?

ROLAND—I wasn't planning to stay long anyway.

GROENEWOADE—Always the young strangers.

ROLAND—*(Extending his hand)* I've enjoyed being your neighbor. Sorry if I disturbed you.

GROENEWOADE—No disturbance at all. *(Shaking his hand)* I got used to your music. I enjoyed hearing you play. You play well.

ROLAND—Thank you.

GROENEWOADE—Always the same piece. Something by Elgar, no?

ROLAND—Yes! You know your music. Concerto in E minor.

GROENEWOADE—You should play maybe something by Dvorak sometime.

ROLAND—I get a feeling for a place. Your street said Elgar.

GROENEWOADE—It will be quiet now. Maybe too quiet.

ROLAND—I'm sorry to be missing the chance to play for another of your psychodramas.

GROENEWOADE—No more psychodramas. Psychodramas are over.

ROLAND—Oh, I'm sorry. So many people used to come.

GROENEWOADE—*(Waving as if to dismiss them)* Tomorrow I put up a sign. No more psychodrama.

ROLAND—*(Shouldering his cello case again)* Well, everything must come to an end, I guess.

GROENEWOADE—Where are the rest of your things? Have you no suitcase?

ROLAND—*(Patting the case now slung over a shoulder)* This is it. Everything I own. I'm wearing all my clothes and carrying all my goods.

GROENEWOADE— The young travel light.

ROLAND—*(Tapping his head)* It's what we carry inside that weighs us down.

GROENEWOADE—*(Nodding)* So it is… So it is…

ROLAND—If I'm ever in this city again, I'll look you up.

GROENEWOADE—Good luck, young man.

(Pidark suddenly meows loudly from inside the cat-carrier. ROLAND *looks down, grinning.)*

ROLAND—You and your cats! *(Turning to wave as he walks away)* Goodbye, Doctor!

*(*DR GROENEWOADE *stands alone, still holding the cat carrier, watching the young man disappear at the end of the block. The street is very quiet. A moment passes as he stands there, glancing*

slowly about. Finally he sets the carrier on the sidewalk and kneels stiffly before it.)

GROENWOADE—*(Opening the carrier and peering inside)* Come on, kitty. Come out, kitty. *(Making cat-calling sounds)* Come on, kitty. *(The white cat cautiously emerges. Gathering him in his arms, Doctor Groenewoade stands again, rubbing his head.)* Ready to go home, kitty? Did you have a good visit? What a good kitty you were, keeping Eleanor company till Jelly Bean came back. *(Kneeling again, he sets him back on the ground.)* Time to go home, kitty. *(As Pidark hesitates)* Go on, kitty. You know the way from here. You can find your way home. *(The cat rubs up against his ankles, in no hurry to go anywhere.)* No, no, kitty. We've got to go. Everybody's got to go now. *(He gives the cat a little shove, who immediately flops over on his side and tries to play with his hand. Doctor Groenewoade ruffles him briefly, then stands. He picks up the cat carrier and closes the door again as he stares down at the cat.)* You're just not going to do what anyone wants, are you?

(As he stands there, a car drives past, startling Pidark back to his feet. Finally he ambles away. As he does, the stage slowly darkens, leaving DR GROENEWOADE *staring after the cat, and begins turning again.)*

Curtain

ACT THREE Scene Five

DuPont Circle, a park in the neighborhood
Saturday night, the next weekend

As DR GROENEWOADE *walk off-stage in the previous scene, the lights dim and come back up to the opening bars of "Today" by the Jefferson Airplane, revealing the fountain in DuPont Circle on a weekend night during the Sixties. The park is crowded with people from the suburbs who have come to the city to experience what's happening. To accommodate them, the city has installed high-school-style stadium lights, flooding the crowd with their glare as though the park were a prison-yard.*

The fountain consists of an upper bowl supported on a column decorated by larger-than-life figures sculpted in white stone, each personifying a different aspect of the ocean: wind, waves and stars. A second, larger basin, formed by a raised rim, collects the water splashing from above. The rim is crowded by the young people who have made this their weekly gathering spot.

Above and behind the fountain, in the dark out of reach of the flood lights, KEVIN *and his band are performing. I never saw a band in DuPont Circle, but if any had played there, they would have played on a stage set up off to one side. Here however the Blues Poodles are presented as playing on a stage set up in the dark above the fountain.*

The entire scene consists in the performance of "Today," by KEVIN *and his band. Beneath them, the crowd of suburbanites stand on a section of the stage that continues to slowly revolve. These figures stand motionless as the stage carries them around, holding postures typical of a cocktail party, or in the act of walking. They are dressed in shades of white and gray. In their midst rises the fountain. The lower basin, with the young people thronging its rim, is on raised ground, clearly visible in their rag-tag outfits and colorful costumes behind the gray crowd.*

Enter PAM PARKER, *walking against the revolution of the stage. She does not so much "enter" as step out from behind another member of the crowd, so that when we first see her, she is already walking in the middle of the scene. Her hair is down again and she is alone in the crowd wearing a colorful pop-art dress. She seems to be the only one who hears the music, and she alone is in motion (though she always remains center stage), picking her way through the crowd.*

She does not appear to see KEVIN *above her, but the music has her in its grip.* KEVIN *does however see her and is obviously singing to her.*

NOTE: This scene is a choreographed whole: the music is the song by the Jefferson Airplane; the dancers consist of the crowd of suburbanites, the young people seated on the fountain and PAM PARKER.

As the song ends, the stage darkens, revolving once more into the play's final scene

Curtain

ACT THREE Scene Six

A highway, somewhere in America
Night

The sound of heavy traffic is heard as the lights come back up, revealing ROLAND LELAND *and* SARAH PANDEL *hitch-hiking together along the side of a road. The cars and trucks roaring past sweep them in the beams of their headlights. A sign above them reads "San Francisco, 2,789 miles."*

ROLAND *is carrying the cello-case on his back and a suitcase that is obviously very heavy in one hand.* SARAH *follows behind him, stylishly dressed in a mini-skirt and go-go boots. She carries a small purse on a strap over her shoulder.*

SARAH—*(Noticing the sign)* Hey, I thought we were going to New York. I want to see Ali again.

ROLAND—You will.

SARAH—The sign says San Francisco.

ROLAND—We're going *by way of* San Francisco.

SARAH—Isn't that a little *out* of the way?

ROLAND—When you travel with me, nothing's out of the way.

SARAH—You're still looking for that girl-friend of yours, aren't you?

ROLAND—No, not anymore…

SARAH—How come? What happened?

ROLAND—Things changed.

SARAH—Then why are we going to San Francisco?

ROLAND—*(Setting the suitcase down and swinging his arm. He does not answer her question.)* Whew, that medicine of yours! What do you have in this, a whole pharmacy?

SARAH—*(Stopping beside him)* My medicine's in my purse.

ROLAND—*(This comes as news)* What's in the suitcase then, rocks?

SARAH—Nothing. Clothes. The book I'm reading.

ROLAND—You're bringing a book?

SARAH—I'm bringing the book I'm reading, yes.

ROLAND—Like this is just one a big vacation where you're going to have time to read?

SARAH—I don't want to lose my place.

ROLAND—What book is it?

SARAH—"Quiet Flows the Don."

ROLAND—*(To himself)* Shit. I'm lugging a Russian novel.

SARAH—And the other two books in the series.

ROLAND—It's a series?

SARAH —"The Don Flows Home to the Sea" and "The Don Keeps on Flowing Home to the Sea."

ROLAND—No wonder it's so heavy!

SARAH—Every year Vivian and I made an agreement to read a certain number of books. You wouldn't want me to go back on my agreement, would you?

ROLAND—I thought you told me she was dead?

SARAH—*I'm* not!

ROLAND—*(Grasping the suitcase again)* I ought to make *you* carry this.

SARAH—I can't. My heart, remember?

ROLAND—*(Extending his thumb again)* As if I could forget!

SARAH—Do you want to know what else we agreed to read?

ROLAND—Three Russian novels aren't enough?

SARAH—"War and Peace," "Dead Souls" and "The Possessed" by Dostoyevsky.

ROLAND—Oh, so it's the year of the Russians, is it? *(Then it hits him.)* No, not…? *(pointing to the suitcase. As SARAH nods)* Jesus, you're bringing a fucking library!

SARAH—Only "The Possessed" is a library book. The rest don't have to be returned.

ROLAND—*(His body goes limp with consternation, then, star-*

ing out into the traffic a moment, trying to remember something) Wait a minute… "The Possessed"…? Isn't that the one where that dissolute aristocrat, what's his name, Stavrogin…?

SARAH—Don't tell me. I don't want to know how it ends.

ROLAND— …Rapes a twelve-year-old girl…?

SARAH—I said don't tell me—

ROLAND—And she hangs herself…?

SARAH—*(Giving him a shove)* You're ruining it for me!

ROLAND—Then *he* hangs *him*self…?

SARAH—Stop! You don't know what you're talking about!

ROLAND— … In a closet—

SARAH—*(Reaching for his mouth)* QUIET!

(The honking of a car-horn behind them interrupts their scuffle. Both turn to look. A car has stopped and is waiting for them. ROLAND waves)

ROLAND—Finally, a ride! *(As they run toward it)* Come on!

(The stage darkens leaving only the sweeping headlights that fade away too as ROLAND and SARAH disappear running along the road.)

Curtain

POSTSCRIPT

POSTSCRIPT *(Optional)*

The projector starts running again and the screen lights up on the dark stage. Above images of the actors, the following postscripts appear:

Kevin and Pam were married in 1968 and had three children. Though Kevin's band never got a record contract and Pam never made partner, eventually Kevin worked his way up to CFO at a public relations firm, and Pam, when the children were grown, took a job at a social justice organization.

Preston Murphy died in 1971 of a new, hither-to unknown disease.

Felix Groenewoade was discovered dead one evening when Maher Kessler arrived for an appointment. The apartment was full of cats and the good Doctor was at his desk, slumped over, wearing only his underwear. Foul play was not suspected.

Eleanor Glass moved to a nursing home where she eventually died.

After sojourning in Denver and San Francisco, Sarah and Roland were later seen together in Monterrey, Mexico. This would have been in the mid Seventies. No one has seen either of them since, though a back-up singer and bass player fitting their description occasionally appeared around the music scenes in Los Angeles, New York and Nashville.

Doctor Heidenreich, after being extradited to Germany, was convicted for his activities during the war and died in prison.

Doctor Groenewoade's house was finally renovated and converted to condominiums. This happened in the Nineteen-Nineties. Starting prices for a one-bedroom were in the low 500's.

www.ingramcontent.com/pod-product-compliance
Lightning Source LLC
Chambersburg PA
CBHW051804040426
42446CB00007B/509